Docker Unveiled

The Comprehensive Handbook to Streamlined Development

William Drake

© **Copyright 2023 - All rights reserved.**

The content contained within this book may not be reproduced, duplicated or transmitted without direct written permission from the author or the publisher.

Under no circumstances will any blame or legal responsibility be held against the publisher, or author, for any damages, reparation, or monetary loss due to the information contained within this book, either directly or indirectly.

<u>Legal Notice:</u>

This book is copyright protected. It is only for personal use. You cannot amend, distribute, sell, use, quote or paraphrase any part, or the content within this book, without the consent of the author or publisher.

<u>Disclaimer Notice:</u>

Please note the information contained within this document is for educational and entertainment purposes only. All effort has been executed to present accurate, up to date, reliable, complete information. No warranties of any kind are declared or implied. Readers acknowledge that the author is not engaging in the rendering of legal, financial, medical or professional advice. The content within this book has been derived from various sources. Please consult a licensed professional before attempting any techniques outlined in this book.

By reading this document, the reader agrees that under no circumstances is the author responsible for any losses, direct or indirect, that are incurred as a result of the use of information contained within this document, including, but not limited to, errors, omissions, or inaccuracies.

TABLE OF CONTENTS

INTRODUCTION

There has never been a more critical demand for speed, consistency, and scalability in the dynamic field of software development. While helpful, traditional approaches may fail when faced with the demands of contemporary applications, leading developers on a never-ending search for improved tools and practices. Presenting Docker: an application packaging, shipping, and running platform that efficiently runs apps as lightweight containers. With its ability to simplify and revolutionize software development and deployment processes, Docker has risen to prominence in the computer sector and is now a vital tool for developers everywhere.

With regard to this innovative technology, "Docker Unveiled: The Comprehensive Handbook to Streamlined Development" seeks to be your go-to resource. This e-book is designed with developers curious about containerization in mind, as well as newcomers starting their Docker journey. We will examine the fundamental ideas behind containerization, comprehend the basic architecture of Docker, and delve deeply into its extensive feature set.

By the time you complete this e-book, you will have a firm understanding of Docker's features and be able to use them to streamline, expedite, and improve your development processes.

Furthermore, you will acquire a comprehensive grasp of how Docker fits into the current development and operational ecosystems through the use of real-world case studies and professional perspectives.

Come along on this in-depth exploration of the Docker universe, where applications expand effortlessly, deployments are reliable, and development is effective. Welcome to "Docker Unveiled: The Comprehensive Handbook to Streamlined Development."

CHAPTER I

Understanding Containerization

What is containerization?

Fundamentally, containerization is a contemporary marvel in the field of software development and deployment. It is a leap in technology that allows programmers and administrators to package an application and all of its dependencies into a standardized setting called a "container." This paradigm change has eliminated the long-standing boundary between operations and development, streamlining the software lifecycle process and resolving the age-old complaint that "it works on my machine!"

Isolating an application in a running environment, independent of the container's host, is the fundamental idea behind containerization. Containerization isolates at the application layer as opposed to typical virtualization techniques, which separate real hardware into numerous instances of virtual machines, each running its own full operating system. This guarantees that all software operates in the same environment, whether it is deployed on a production server hosted in the cloud or on a developer's laptop.

The distinctive feature of containerization lies in its capacity to bundle an application with all of its runtime components, such as binaries, libraries, and configuration files. This encapsulation removes discrepancies caused by different program versions or system configurations and guarantees consistency. This eliminates the need for developers to deal with problems brought on by differences between the development, staging, and production environments. Applications now come with all of their dependencies, simplifying deployment and eliminating the need for labor-intensive environment setup and configuration for operations teams.

But consistency and encapsulation aren't the only benefits of containerization. Owing to their low weight, containers are very effective. Instead of starting up an entire OS, they share the host system's OS kernel, which lowers overhead and speeds up startup times. Because of this, containers have become particularly appealing for microservices designs, in which programs are divided into discrete, standalone services that function as separate entities. In these kinds of situations, the flexibility of containers enables the autonomous development, scaling, and management of every microservice.

Moreover, containerization adds a level of portability that was not possible before. A containerized program can be easily transported from a developer's workstation to a test environment, and finally to a cloud provider, all while maintaining consistency of functionality. Software delivery pipelines become more agile and quick due to this portability, which reduces the complexity that frequently results from variances in infrastructure.

It is impossible to discuss containerization without mentioning Docker's crucial contribution—a platform that made it popular. Organizations are finding it easier to implement containerization due to Docker's user-friendly interface, large image collection, and orchestration toolkit. Although Kubernetes, a platform for container orchestration, and containerd, a container runtime, add layers of functionality and enable more complex use cases, Docker continues to be the main player in the container ecosystem.

It's important to realize that containerization, despite all of its benefits, is not a panacea for every software deployment issue. Like any other technology, it has a learning curve and complexities. For example, further attention may be required when containerizing stateful apps, which necessitate a persistent data back-end. Furthermore, security is still an issue with containers, just like it is with any shared environment. Best practices, frequent upgrades, and careful monitoring are required to keep containers safe.

Containerization, in conclusion, is a big step toward reliable, effective, and portable software deployment. Its capacity to contain programs within a uniform setting has completely changed how we create, test, and implement software. Although it has some drawbacks, its advantages in terms of effectiveness, consistency, and portability are not denied. With its promise of rapid procedures and faster deployments, containerization is poised to become a fundamental component of modern software architectures as we approach a software-defined future.

Advantages of containerized applications

Containerization has become a revolutionary thread in the complex tapestry of contemporary software development and deployment, changing how we design, develop, and distribute programs. As we examine this paradigm further, we see that containerized apps have numerous benefits that simplify processes across the technical, operational, and financial domains, making them a vital tool in the modern digital environment.

The significant influence that containerization has on consistency is among its most well-known advantages. For many years, developers and operators have struggled with the age-old problem of differences between development, staging, and production environments. "It works on my machine" became a standard response, with many deployment problems being attributed to underlying environmental variations. Containerization has successfully addressed this issue by combining apps with the required runtime environment. An application's environment travels with it when it is containerized, guaranteeing consistent operation wherever the container is deployed. This encapsulation facilitates more seamless development-to-production transfers by avoiding uncertainty and lowering deployment failure rates.

Optimization of resources and efficiency are additional distinguishing features. Conventional virtualization techniques can be resource-intensive since they involve running several instances of fully functional operating systems on top of a hypervisor. In contrast, application processes are isolated from one another and share the host OS kernel in containers. This method minimizes overhead because it eliminates the need to operate several OS instances. As such, containers are lighter than virtual machines (VMs), start up more quickly, and frequently outperform them in terms of performance. Because of its efficiency, a single server may support more containers than virtual machines, which improves resource efficiency and lowers costs.

And there's the benefit of flexibility and scalability. In order to adapt to changing demands, modern applications—particularly those with microservices architectures—must scale out quickly. Because they are lightweight, containers can be instantiated promptly, facilitating simple and speedy horizontal scaling. This scalability is about agility as much as being able to handle additional traffic. According to the requirements of an application, developers can quickly construct, destroy, replace, or duplicate containers, which speeds up the continuous integration and deployment (CI/CD) and rapid iterative development processes.

Applications that are containerized are more appealing due to their portability. An application loses its independence from its deployment environment once it has been containerized. This implies that a developer's laptop, a test environment, a data center, or a cloud infrastructure can all execute the same container without any issues. Because of this portability, migrations, upgrades, and rollbacks are easier to handle because the usual obstacles brought about by differences in underlying infrastructures are removed. It also allows companies to implement multi-cloud strategies without being constrained by platform-specific requirements.

Containerization improves security from an operational standpoint by adding an additional isolation layer. Because each program operates in its own isolated environment, any vulnerabilities or failures in one container won't affect the others. Although container security is a large field that needs constant attention, the intrinsic isolation offers a first line of defense against some threats.

Furthermore, the benefits of containerized applications have expanded further with the emergence of container orchestration tools such as Kubernetes. By managing containerized apps' networking, scaling, deployment, and maintenance, these platforms enable enterprises to operate complicated applications across machine clusters easily. Businesses can guarantee high availability, effective resource allocation, and smooth scaling with such technologies at their disposal, strengthening the case for containerization's advantages.

Containerization has strong benefits in terms of economy. Cost reductions are directly correlated with resource efficiency since it allow firms to maximize hardware use. Containerized workflows' speed and agility can shorten time-to-market and give businesses a competitive edge. Additionally, containers can result in significant savings in terms of lowered troubleshooting times and minimal downtime by guaranteeing consistency and lowering deployment failure rates.

In conclusion, containerized programs are a combination of economic prudence, consistency, efficiency, scalability, portability, and security. With the software ecosystem constantly changing and expectations for high availability, faster delivery times, and seamless user experiences, containerization stands out as a beacon that points developers and companies toward an increasingly robust, agile, and efficient future.

Comparison with virtualization

When discussing software deployment and scalability in the dynamic field of modern computing, the terms virtualization and containerization frequently come up together. Although both technologies aim to encapsulate applications in isolated environments, there are significant differences between their methodologies, underlying processes, and application domains. Analyzing these technologies' complexities provides a unique viewpoint on how software deployment has changed over time and the procedures that support it.

In the field of IT, virtualization has been a constant for many years. Hardware simulation is used to build several separate virtual machines (or VMs) on a single physical server. On top of a hypervisor, each virtual machine (VM) runs its whole operating system (OS), including the kernel and user-space components. This hypervisor abstracts and allots the server's physical resources to these virtual machines (VMs). It can be either a hosted type (Type 2), like Oracle's VirtualBox, or a bare-metal type (Type 1), like VMware's ESXi. As such, virtual machines (VMs) operate independently of one another, even while they share a machine with other VMs.

Virtualization's ability to optimize resource consumption is one of its most appealing features. Organizations can optimize hardware utilization, cut costs, and simplify management by consolidating various operating systems onto fewer servers instead of having several underutilized physical servers. Virtual machines also provide strong isolation. Assuring resilience and security, a failure or security breach in one virtual machine does not automatically jeopardize others. Because of these benefits, virtualization helped to establish the foundation for early cloud computing by enabling service providers to safely and effectively serve several clients from a single server.

Despite being a relatively new concept, containerization has drastically changed how programs are created, implemented, and expanded. Containerization isolates at the application level as opposed to virtualization's hardware-level isolation. An application and all of its dependencies—such as libraries, binaries, and configuration files—are bundled together into a single unit using containers. It is important to note that while each container on a host has its own user space, they all share the same OS kernel. Because of this design principle, containers are lightweight, starting almost instantly and requiring less resources than virtual machines (VMs).

Though it's easy to view containerization as just virtualization's more effective replacement, there's more to it than that. An unparalleled degree of consistency is achieved through containers. Containers solve the long-standing issue of environmental disparities by combining applications with their dependencies, guaranteeing that applications function consistently across various infrastructures. This uniformity decreases deployment errors, streamlines debugging, and speeds up development workflows. Furthermore, the concepts of microservices and continuous integration and deployment are perfectly aligned with containers' transient nature, allowing them to be instantiated and destroyed quickly.

On the other hand, it is crucial to understand that virtualization and containerization are not mutually exclusive. In numerous situations, they may work in tandem. For example, containers can operate inside virtual machines (VMs) to use the agility of containers and the strong isolation of virtualization. In multi-tenant settings where security is crucial, this fusion becomes very important.

The lightweight nature of containers and their lack of a complete OS stack gives them an advantage in terms of performance. But virtual machines don't share the OS kernel, so they provide more reliable isolation. Therefore, containers may be preferred in dynamic application contexts for quick scalability, but virtual machines (VMs) may be selected when robust workload separation is of utmost importance.

Overall, both ecosystems have reached remarkable maturity in terms of orchestration and management. The virtualization space offers complete solutions for complex virtual machine lifecycles management, such as VMware vSphere and Microsoft Hyper-V. On the other hand, orchestration solutions such as Kubernetes, which control the networking, scaling, and deployment of containers amongst clusters, dominate the container landscape.

In conclusion, the argument between virtualization and containerization is about appropriateness rather than superiority.

Every technology has carved out a niche for itself due to unique requirements and difficulties in the IT industry. Virtualization is still a reliable workhorse for many businesses because of its history and strong isolation. In the meantime, containerization is changing contemporary software development and deployment paradigms with its promises of agility, consistency, and resource efficiency. In the complex web of modern computers, it is critical to comprehend the advantages, nuances, and uses of both technologies.

CHAPTER II

Docker: An Overview

History and inception of Docker

Throughout the history of software development, some ideas have sparked significant changes that have changed the way we design, create, and implement applications. Among these revolutionary forces, Docker stands out with its simple whale logo. It is necessary to navigate the narrow paths of Docker's origins, history, and ascent to become the giant of containerization to understand its influence fully.

The history of Docker begins in the early 2010s and is centered on the dotCloud startup, which Solomon Hykes co-founded. Containerization wasn't a problem for DotCloud at first. Rather, it was a Platform-as-a-Service (PaaS) provider, emphasizing helping developers host and grow online applications. Nonetheless, the dotCloud team's new approach—containerization—was prompted by the difficulties in maintaining consistent environments throughout the application's lifetime. Their goal was to contain programs in separate, standardized environments so that they would behave the same way everywhere they were deployed.

Docker was first presented to the public by Solomon Hykes at the PyCon conference in March 2013. Although the program used already-existing container technologies, namely Linux Containers (LXC), its innovative feature was how easy it was to use. It abstracted away a large portion of the complexity involved in container operations by providing a straightforward command-line interface and an API for building, maintaining, and executing containers. However, Docker offered a fresh method for creating container images and was more than just an LXC wrapper. Layering Docker images allowed for versioning and reuse, significantly decreasing the overhead and setup time for environments.

The Docker community gained popularity quite quickly. Developers became aware of its many advantages, including consistency between environments, lower overhead compared to virtual machines (VMs), and the ability to encapsulate all dependencies within containers, which eliminated the infamous "it works on my machine" issue. The choice of Docker to become open source, which lets the larger community improve and enhance its features, accelerated its acceptance even more.

Docker had already come to represent containerization by 2014. Having seen the tool's potential and wanting to change the direction of its business plan, dotCloud changed its name to Docker Inc. At this same period, Docker started to separate from LXC and create its own container runtime known as "libcontainer." With this change, Docker could communicate directly with the Linux kernel, giving it more flexibility and preventing it from being tied to a particular container technology.

The Docker ecosystem had an explosion in the years after its founding. With the introduction of the Docker Hub, a cloud-based registry service, developers could now exchange and distribute container images. This functioned as a repository, similar to GitHub but for Docker images, facilitating application environment reuse and fostering collaboration. As more and more containers with interdependencies were used in real-world applications, Docker's ascent also sparked interest in its orchestration. As a result, technologies like Docker Swarm for clustering and orchestration and Docker Compose for creating multi-container applications were released.

Although Docker's impact was evident, there were difficulties along the way. There was fierce rivalry in the container orchestration space, particularly from Google's Kubernetes project. Docker Swarm was subsequently eclipsed by Kubernetes' all-encompassing approach to coordinating containerized workloads, leading Docker Inc. to include Kubernetes support into its platform by 2017.

Docker has made numerous contributions to the software ecosystem despite competitive obstacles. 'Infrastructure as Code,' where environments are versioned and controlled similarly to software code, gained popularity with its ascent. Docker ensures consistency from development to production, leading to a resurgence of the Continuous Integration and Continuous Deployment (CI/CD) pipelines. Given that Docker can encapsulate each service in its own container, microservices architectures—which divide programs into smaller, independently deployable components—also found a natural ally in the platform.

In conclusion, Docker's evolution from a side project inside a PaaS firm to a vital component of contemporary software deployment is evidence of its transformational potential. Despite its foundation in pre-existing container technology, Docker's genius was in the democratization, abstraction, and simplification of containerization. Thinking back to its origins and history, Docker has become more than just a tool—instead, it's a movement that has completely changed how we think about software development, deployment, and scalability. Its history is firmly established as a sign of reliability, effectiveness, and adaptability in the rapidly changing software industry, regardless of future technical developments.

Docker's architecture (Docker daemon, Docker client, Docker registries)

A significant factor in Docker's explosive growth in the software deployment space has been its dependable and user-friendly architecture. Docker's design is brilliant because of its layered, modular structure, which guarantees scalability and flexibility. The Docker Daemon, Docker Client, and Docker Registries make up the trinity that forms the foundation of Docker's architecture. By breaking down these components, we can learn more about the fundamental ideas and working mechanisms underlying Docker's containerization abilities.

Let's start by exploring the Docker Daemon, the main engine underlying Docker's features. The Docker Daemon, or just "Dockerd," is a persistent background process that oversees Docker containers on a system. The central nervous system manages vital functions like constructing, operating, and planning containers. Because of its critical function, the Daemon must directly connect with the operating system's underlying capabilities, using system libraries and kernel features—particularly those associated with containerization, such as Linux's namespaces and cgroups.

Additionally, the Docker Daemon makes available a REST API, which is a crucial interface through which other Docker tools can interact with the Daemon and coordinate container operations. Docker's modular architecture is illustrated by this API-driven design, which permits different components to work together harmoniously while yet having separate roles.

Turning away from the Daemon, we come upon the Docker Client, which is the user's main Docker interface. Developers and operators engage with the Docker Client when they issue commands such as "docker run" or "docker build." But the Client doesn't carry out these duties by itself. Rather, it serves as a conduit, converting these commands into the proper API calls that the Docker Daemon receives and executes to complete the necessary tasks.

Docker Client and Docker Daemon interactions might occur on the same host or on different hosts connected via networks. This adaptability highlights Docker's distributed nature, enabling various configurations where developers can orchestrate container activities across machines or even data centers using a local client to communicate with remote Daemons.

Docker Registries complete the architectural triad and are essential to distributing and archiving Docker images. Consider Docker images to be blueprints that hold the runtime configurations, dependencies, and applications. Registries ensure that images are efficiently saved and retrieved for various purposes such as sharing, scaling, and deployment.

Perhaps the most well-known registry is Docker Hub, which Docker Inc runs. It is a sizable public repository where developers may push and pull images, promoting reuse and cooperation. Nevertheless, Docker Hub is not the only place where Docker Registries exist. AWS Elastic Container Registry and Google Container Registry are two more public registries. Additionally, companies can create private registries, guaranteeing that their confidential or proprietary Docker images stay inside the company and offer another degree of protection and control.

A Docker Client initially performs a local check before issuing a command to launch a container from an image. The client will then attempt to contact the configured registry, retrieve the necessary image, and direct the Docker Daemon to instantiate a container if the image is unavailable. From local search to registry retrieval, this smooth process highlights the effectiveness and connectivity built into Docker's architecture.

Docker's architecture essentially reflects the modularity, adaptability, and user-centricity concepts that have been the foundation of its success. With its management role and close ties to the operating system, the Docker Daemon ensures that containers are orchestrated effectively. With its simple command-line interface, the Docker Client allows users to manage and communicate with Docker without becoming bogged down in details. Additionally, the Docker Registries guarantee that applications packaged as Docker images may be easily shared, scaled, and deployed due to their crucial role in image distribution and storage.

In conclusion, Docker's architectural genius is not limited to its elements but is found in the symphony they create when combined. Like a well-oiled machine, every component works in unison to accomplish the overall goal of streamlining and democratizing containerization, which is what Docker is all about. Thus, by comprehending its design, we can appreciate the workings of Docker and its goal: a universally accessible, efficient, and consistent software deployment environment.

Docker objects: images, containers, networks, and volumes

Docker is a master craftsman in the field of containerization, building complex, scalable, and reliable application environments. But in order to fully understand Docker's potential, we must examine its objects, which are its essential building elements. The solid and adaptable base of Docker's containerized ecosystems comprises several objects: images, containers, networks, and volumes.

Docker's orchestration revolves around the idea of images. Like a blueprint or template, a Docker image contains all of an application's dependencies, libraries, and configurations. A snapshot that is static and unchangeable, an image defines the environment in which an application will operate. They contain all the necessary components to initiate a process, guaranteeing that the dreaded "it works on my machine" dilemma is rendered obsolete. Once specified, these images can be easily shared, distributed, and versioned by being kept in private repositories or registries like Docker Hub.

The dynamic world of containers arises from the static domain of images. A container is the realized structure, the living embodiment of an image, if an image represents a blueprint. A container is created by Docker when it instantiates an image. A container is a runnable instance of an application that shares the OS kernel of the underlying host while being isolated in its environment. Containers are transient in nature; they are meant to be quickly constructed, altered, and discarded. This transient character fits particularly well with contemporary software paradigms, requiring resilient, scalable, and agile programs, such as microservices and continuous deployment. It's important to remember that although images cannot be altered after they are instantiated, containers can. They may also be committed to creating new images, enabling iterative development and deployment.

We explore Docker's architecture in further detail and come upon the complex network architecture. Even though they are separate, containers are uncommon in solitary confinement. In real-world applications, it is common for several containers to interact, cooperate, and perform different tasks simultaneously. This inter-container communication is made efficient and secure by Docker's networking objects. Several network configurations are available by default with Docker, including bridge (which leverages the host's private internal network), host (which makes use of the host's networking), and overlay (which connects multiple Docker daemons). Users can specify custom networks in addition to these defaults, giving them more precise control over how containers interact. This modularity guarantees that Docker's networking capabilities can handle the interplay skillfully, regardless of the type of application—from a straightforward standalone to a sophisticated multi-container arrangement covering many hosts.

Now that we have finished investigating Docker's objects, we are in the world of volumes. Although containers are incredibly flexible, their transient nature makes durable data storage more challenging. Once a container is destroyed, any data contained inside will be lost. In this case, volumes become Docker's means of managing and storing persistent data. An assigned volume is a data storage location controlled by Docker and exists independently of the container. By mounting Docker volumes to containers, it is possible to transfer data between several containers and guarantee that sensitive data, such as databases, is preserved during the container's lifecycle. Docker's volume management also offers features like volume migration, backup, and restoration, guaranteeing data flexibility and integrity.

In conclusion, Docker's containerized ecosystems are supported by diverse components, each of which plays a crucial part, even though they appear seamless on the surface. Applications and their surroundings are guaranteed to be uniformly defined and versioned due to images. These images are given life via containers, which offer isolated, executable instances of applications. These containers are connected by networks, which guarantee secure and efficient communication. And volumes protect the information, ensuring longevity in the fleeting dance of containers. When combined, these items represent Docker's vision of a world where building comprehensive, scalable, and resilient environments is just as important to software deployment as writing code, allowing applications to flourish rather than just run.

CHAPTER III

Setting Up Docker

Prerequisites for Docker installation

Developers are faced with many options when it comes to tools and platforms in the current software world. However, Docker consistently stands out due to its promise of simplified containerization. However, the elegance of Docker in action is based on meticulous backstage preparations, just like any excellent performance. One must ensure the system satisfies specific requirements before installing and using Docker efficiently. In addition to laying the groundwork for a seamless Docker installation, we also learn more about the design and operational principles that support this revolutionary tool by investigating these fundamental needs.

Let's start by recognizing a basic principle: Docker and the operating system are intrinsically coupled. Docker, initially created for Linux, uses namespaces and cgroups among other capabilities to manage resources and isolate processes. Because of this fundamental link, installing Docker requires a supported operating system as a prerequisite. Although the standard platforms have been Linux distributions like Ubuntu, CentOS, and Debian, Docker's expanding design has made it more versatile. Current Docker versions can be installed on Windows and macOS, however, it's important to note that Docker adds an abstraction layer by running on top of a virtualized Linux kernel on these operating systems. Consequently, selecting a native Linux environment typically pays off in terms of simplicity and performance, particularly for production installations.

After navigating the OS space, focus turns to hardware. Docker is a lightweight technology, but the containers it manages shape the needs it must meet. At the very least, Systems should have a 64-bit processor and 4GB of RAM. This need is essential since Docker images and containers are made for 64-bit architectures. Although it may seem small, the amount of RAM needed might increase depending on containerized programs. A program that uses a lot of databases, for example, would require a lot more memory. Comparably, storage considerations need to consider image sizes, volume data, and container filesystems, even though a basic 20GB guideline is a good place to start. Users need to assess the requirements of their applications and make sure the hardware is not only suitable but also expandable.

After the foundations of OS and hardware are established, the emphasis shifts to particular software requirements. The operating system version is a crucial factor to take into account. Because of its quick progress, Docker frequently requires newer OS updates to guarantee security and compatibility. For Linux users, this means that Docker's container features require a more recent version of the kernel, preferably 3.10 or above. Furthermore, because Docker depends on features like Hyper-V, a virtualization technology, to virtualize the Linux kernel, enabling them on platforms like Windows becomes essential. Docker Desktop on macOS requires virtualization to be enabled, which is a capability that most recent Macs come with by default.

The package manager is an essential piece of software for Docker installation, even aside from OS details. Users of Linux may be familiar with dnf for Fedora, yum for CentOS, or apt for Ubuntu. By obtaining the necessary packages from repositories and managing dependencies, these package managers make installing Docker easier. The official Docker literature frequently offers instructions and scripts designed specifically for various package managers, expediting installation. It's important to remember that installing Docker may require multiple components, including the command-line interface (CLI), Docker Compose (which orchestrates applications using several containers), and Docker Engine (which is the main runtime). Every element may have requirements, emphasizing the importance of carefully reading official paperwork.

Even though it sounds basic, network connectivity is another essential requirement. Pulling images from registries, updating components, and occasionally interacting with cloud services are all part of Docker's workflow. That's why having a reliable internet connection—preferably one with fast speed—is essential. Furthermore, because Docker activities may require downloading huge images, bandwidth and data restrictions are important to consider, particularly in environments with limited resources or when doing bulk operations.

In the context of Docker, security is both necessary and essential. Contemporary operating systems are pre-configured with security modules such as AppArmor or SELinux. These techniques strengthen system security but can also interfere with Docker in unanticipated ways, making container operations more difficult. It is crucial to ensure that these security modules have whitelisted or properly configured Docker's installation and runtime procedures. Similarly, firewalls— essential to system defenses—must be set up to let Docker's daemon and API processes provide unimpeded intra- and inter-container communication.

In conclusion, although the seamless containerization that Docker promises to deliver is what makes it so alluring, getting there requires careful planning. Docker's installation requires careful attention to detail, including hardware concerns to operating system quirks, program versions, and security setups. Nonetheless, there are benefits to this level of detail. We don't simply simplify Docker installation by ensuring prerequisites are satisfied; we also create the environment for secure, scalable, and optimal container operations. Docker's performance in the vast theater of software deployment is captivating, but it also has many unsung backstage preparations to thank for its success. Furthermore, as we successfully complete these requirements, we become more than just viewers—instead, we empower and co-author the Docker revolution.

Installation steps for different OS (Windows, MacOS, Linux)

The pioneer of containerization, Docker, is still transforming software development and deployment environments. Its promise to encapsulate applications in lightweight, consistent, and standardized environments is appealing to users of various operating systems, including MacOS, Windows, and Linux, all of which are known for their resilience. Although Docker's philosophy is the same for all of these operating systems, the installation process differs depending on the subtleties and complexity of each platform. As we set out on our adventure, we'll learn how to apply Docker's magic to Linux, MacOS, and Windows, and we'll come to appreciate Docker's unique combination of customization and universality.

The Windows ecosystem was historically seen as an outsider to the native Docker experience due to its large user base. But because to Docker's development and Microsoft's adoption of open-source concepts, Docker is now comfortable on Windows. Ensuring the system is prepared is the first step in the journey. Current Docker versions rely on the virtualization technology found in Windows 10's Hyper-V functionality. Thus, it is essential to make sure that one's version of Windows supports Hyper-V and that it is turned on. Furthermore, a 64-bit version of Docker for Windows with at least the Pro or Enterprise versions is required.

Once system compatibility has been verified, it's easy to use Docker Desktop, the official Docker tool for Windows. Installing Docker Desktop is a simple process and is available on the official Docker website. Docker launches with a straightforward installer download and the well-known "next-next-finish" sequence. After installation, the user can launch their first containerized application with just a terminal command once the Docker icon in the taskbar indicates that it is operational. The potential to switch between Linux and Windows containers is one notable feature of Docker on Windows, which is a credit to both Docker's adaptability and Windows' growing openness.

Because of its Unix foundations, the MacOS universe offers Docker a rich environment. But on MacOS, Docker runs on top of a virtualized Linux kernel, just like it does on Windows. Virtualization is built into recent Mac hardware, so one must confirm that their Mac supports it before beginning the installation process. Furthermore, Docker Desktop for Mac emphasizes the necessity for reasonably updated software by requiring MacOS Yosemite 10.10.3 or later.

As long as the requirements are met, installation is simple. The well-known DMG file is used to package Docker Desktop for Mac, which can be found on the Docker website. You only need to drag and drop the Docker application into the Applications folder. When you run it from the Applications folder, Docker indicates it's ready to use with an animated icon on the top menu bar. The Docker CLI is a special feature for MacOS users that installs alongside Docker and lets developers and power users work with Docker in a terminal to utilize its capabilities fully. It's also important to note that Docker Desktop has a feature-rich graphical user interface (or GUI) that makes it simple for users of each and every skill levels to manage containers, images, and settings.

The native operating system of Docker, Linux, provides a strong and unadulterated installation experience. Docker installs differently on each Linux distribution due to the fragmented nature of the OS, which includes Fedora, CentOS, Ubuntu, and other types. However, certain universals hold across these distributions. Docker requires a kernel 3.10 or higher and a 64-bit architecture in order for its container features to work as intended.

For those who enjoy Ubuntu, the apt package manager can be used to download Docker from the official repository. A few packages, including docker-ce, docker-ce-cli, and containerd.io, must be obtained before installing Docker, after updating local package information using apt-get update. Followers of Fedora use the dnf package management, and those who prefer CentOS rely on Yum. While the commands vary, the basic idea remains consistent: Update local package metadata, fetch Docker packages, and enable and start the Docker service. The command docker run hello-world, which indicates that Docker has been successfully installed, functions as a test and a rite of passage after installation.

But Linux's configurable nature is what gives it its power. Beyond the basic installation, users can adjust Docker's settings, explore unique storage backends, or even choose more complex setups like Swarm or Docker Compose. Additionally, installation scripts for different distributions are provided in Docker's official documentation, guaranteeing consumers a seamless experience customized for their setup.

In conclusion, Docker's experience with Linux, MacOS, and Windows is evidence of its adaptability and universality. Although every operating system has its own set of difficulties and subtleties, Docker's installation procedure skillfully handles these, guaranteeing that users can take advantage of containerization regardless of their platform preference. The ultimate goal is always the same, whether it's the command-line prowess of Docker on Linux or the GUI elegance of Docker Desktop: providing a seamless, potent, and revolutionary container experience. Through these installation methods, we adopt a philosophy that promotes speed, innovation, and consistency rather than just onboarding a tool.

Verifying the installation

It's not enough to simply follow the installation instructions when it comes to software installations, especially when working with tools as crucial as Docker. Real success is confirmed by the following validation process, which consists of verifying that the tool is on the system and is operating as intended. Checking the performance of an installation is like testing an automobile after maintenance; the actual evidence of the work's success is in how well it performs. This verification phase becomes much more important when using Docker because of the tool's essential function in pipelines for development and deployment. Now, let's set out to ensure that Docker is installed wholly and flawlessly.

It takes a combination of interactive and observational checks to ensure that Docker is successfully setup; installing it is only half the battle. The main goal is to verify Docker's functionality and, consequently, its preparedness to support containerization.

The observational check is the first and easiest verification phase. Users using MacOS and Windows can receive instant visual feedback with Docker Desktop. The first indication that an installation is successful is the appearance of the Docker icon, which is a whale-shaped icon with containers on its back, on the taskbar

(Windows) or menu bar (MacOS). This visual indication is Docker's gateway, not merely an icon. When you click on it, settings, options, and—most importantly—the Docker daemon's current state are displayed. This icon would typically be colored or animated when Docker is operating, indicating that it is active. Though comforting, this visual confirmation is simply the tip of the iceberg.

The real interactive test of Docker's installation is the command-line interface (CLI), which works on Linux, Mac OS, and Windows alike. Equipped with Docker commands, the user assumes the role of the investigator, with the terminal or command prompt serving as the stage. docker --version is the fundamental command that every user should use as a rite of passage. Running this command should yield the version number of Docker, confirming its existence and revealing details about the installed version. Knowing the version helps users stay updated with features, security fixes, and potential deprecations, given Docker's rapid evolution.

When one looks closer, the command docker info is a really useful troubleshooting tool. This tool produces a comprehensive report on the Docker setup, which is more detailed than the version check. It lists the quantity of containers (both running and stopped), the available images, the storage details, and even system information like the kernel version and operating system type. This output provides a wealth of system information that the observant user can use to better understand how Docker interacts with the host environment and serves as validation.

But Docker's real strength lies in its ability to operate containers. Therefore, executing a test container is the last step in validation. Programming language equivalent of a 'Hello, World!' application is Docker's docker run hello-world command. Docker tries to launch a container with the hello-world image when it is executed. It fetches the image from Docker Hub (if it's not locally available) and runs it if it is installed and configured correctly. In addition to confirming Docker's operational condition, the output—a kind greeting from Docker—also guarantees network access to Docker Hub and the sustainability of container operations.

Although the hello-world container is a simple test, more complicated images, such as Ubuntu or Alpine, are an option for individuals seeking a more thorough validation. Docker is tested by running interactive sessions with these images using commands such as docker run -it ubuntu /bin/bash. This confirms that Docker can handle heavier workloads and communicate with popular images.

Moreover, further verification processes are required for customers who have pushed beyond basic Docker deployments. For example, users who have installed Docker Compose could use docker-compose --version to confirm the installation. Likewise, additional features or plugins may include their own set of verification commands, highlighting the necessity of customizing the validation procedure to the scope of the installation.

But it's important to remember that verification involves more than just affirmative confirmations. It's also critical to keep an eye out for mistakes or abnormalities. Because Docker is a system-intensive technology, it may occasionally encounter permissions problems, particularly on Linux. It's critical to ensure the user is added to the docker group or their permissions are set correctly. Similar problems that may arise after installation include network problems, port conflicts, or disparities in storage. A watchful user looks out for potential red flags and approaches the verification procedure as a confirmation and a diagnostic phase.

Essentially, verifying that Docker is installed is a link between the installation process and the skill of using. From the optimism of a successful installation to the assurance of operational preparedness, a shift occurs. Equipped with directives and keen observation, users traversing this bridge provide the foundation for invention, development, and implementation rather than merely verifying a tool. Verification is a prologue to exploration rather than an epilogue to installation in the grand story of containerization.

CHAPTER IV

Docker Images

Understanding Docker images

One fundamental component is at the center of the complex architecture of Docker, where volumes, networks, and containers interact: the Docker image. Docker images, which are more than just digital constructions, are essential to containerization because they are compact, standardized, and portable snapshots of applications. We will explore Docker's fundamental ideas and learn how an image may completely transform software development, deployment, and distribution as we go deeper into the subject of Docker images.

An initial impression of a Docker image may be similar to that of a template or blueprint. Although this is a useful analogy, the image's meaning goes deeper. An application's whole runtime environment, including its code, libraries, environment variables, runtime, and configuration files, is contained in a Docker image. This thorough encapsulation guarantees that the application will function consistently no matter where the Docker image is executed. Consequently, the age-old "it works on my machine" conundrum that has plagued developers for decades is elegantly avoided.

Images are unchangeable. An image cannot have its contents changed once it has been made. Being unchangeable is essential to preserving coherentness. An image that functions on a developer's local computer will perform exactly the same on a test server, a colleague's PC, or even in a worldwide production environment if it is left untouched and unchanged. The development-to-deployment pipeline is streamlined by this predictability, which also removes inconsistencies that are sometimes brought about by environmental variances.

So how does one go about making an image? The Dockerfile is the wonder tool in Docker's toolbox. A script of instructions that tells Docker how to construct an image is called a Dockerfile. The Dockerfile carefully scripts the image generation process, defining everything from the base OS layer (such as Ubuntu or Alpine) to the software to be installed, environment variable settings, file copies, and entry point definitions. A new Docker image that is prepared for distribution or deployment is produced when a user issues the docker build command, which causes Docker to read this Dockerfile and carry out its instructions one after the other.

Another brilliant architectural feature of Docker images is layering. Unlike single-unit objects, Docker images consist of several layers. Generally, a Dockerfile's instructions generate a new layer for each one. The final image is created by stacking these layers one after the other. There are several benefits to this layered strategy. It optimizes storage first. Docker cleverly reuses the base layer if many images share it (for example, the same operating system), avoiding redundancy. Second, layering improves the effectiveness of the build process. Docker uses cached layers to find instructions that haven't changed when a Dockerfile is altered, rebuilding only the impacted layers and those that sit on top of it.

Docker registries make it easier for images to be shared and distributed globally. Docker Hub—the official Docker repository for public images—is the most well-known among them. Developers and organizations may publish their customized images using Docker Hub for public use. Third-party solutions or private registries like Docker Trusted Registry can be employed for more regulated and safe distribution. Upon executing the docker pull command, Docker retrieves the designated image from a registry and saves it locally for utilization. Similarly, the last stage in many pipelines for continuous integration/continuous deployment (CI/CD) is docker push, which uploads a locally accessible image to a registry.

But without knowing the intricate balance that occurs between images and containers, one cannot fully comprehend Docker images. A container is an image's runtime instance, whereas an image is a static snapshot. In object-oriented programming, consider an image as a class with a container as its object. A new container launches and runs the program contained in the image each time the docker run command is used with an image. Additionally, many containers spun from the same image exhibit the same behavior due to the image's immutability, supporting Docker's consistency guarantee.

Additionally, the development of microservices architecture has been accelerated by Docker images because of their comprehensiveness and compactness. Modern software designs frequently break down large programs into smaller services, each contained within its own Docker image. When these images are used as containers, they work together to provide all of the application's features. This modularization improves robustness, scalability, and maintainability and is made possible through Docker images.

In conclusion, Docker images are foundational to containerization because of their uniformity and encapsulation. Their actions exemplify Docker's motto, "Build, Ship, and Run Any App, Anywhere." The larger story becomes evident as developers integrate applications into images and as companies share these images worldwide: Docker images are more than just technological innovations; they are paradigm shifters changing how software is created, distributed, and used. Understanding the depth and breadth of Docker images gives us a peek into the software of the future, which promises unmatched consistency, scalability, and efficiency.

Using Docker Hub

If Docker images are the fundamental building blocks of Docker's containerized world, then Docker Hub serves as the grand repository, a central marketplace, and a distribution hub. It is becoming increasingly important for developers to comprehend and use Docker Hub efficiently as the Docker ecosystem gets more widely adopted. This platform is more than just a storage solution; it embodies containerization's collaborative attitude, encouraging sharing, easy deployment across various settings, and teamwork.

Fundamentally, Docker Hub functions as a cloud-based registry, a virtual safe where Docker images are kept and retrieved. However, just referring to it as a "repository" would be underestimating it. Docker Hub serves as a community hub, a distribution center for the general public, and a haven of information for containerized applications, much like libraries do for books. Whether a developer is looking for a particular image or an organization wants to distribute its works, Docker Hub is frequently the first choice.

Docker Hub's extensive collection of official images is one of its main advantages. These are repositories that Docker or the companies that created the program have verified and are keeping up with. For example, a developer does not have to start from scratch if they want to install a Redis or MySQL instance. Official Docker Hub images for such widely used software solutions are easily accessible. These images may be retrieved with just a docker pull command, guaranteeing simplicity of deployment, optimization, and authenticity assurance.

Official images aren't the only ones available on Docker Hub, though. The platform supports the open-source philosophy and lets companies and individual developers promote their own brands. This democratization makes a plethora of customized solutions, experimental software, and niche tools possible. Anyone using Docker can host a public repository, establish a free account, and share their image with the entire development community online. Peer contributions like these improve the ecosystem, spurring innovation and expanding the range of available tools.

However, the benefit of large repositories also brings with it the difficulty of trust and navigation. Among millions of images, how does one find the appropriate one? Docker Hub's user-friendly search and filtering features help with this. Through keyword searches, popularity, recent updates, and other criteria, users can filter through images. Every repository on Docker Hub also has metadata, including information on the image's description, tags, pull count, last update, and user comments. This metadata directs users during the selection process like a beacon.

Trust is crucial, particularly in the open-source community. Docker Hub's automated builds and star rating system serve to emphasize this further. Repositories can be rated by users, offering a kind of peer endorsement. Higher star ratings are frequently indicative of dependable and widely accepted repositories. Transparency is further ensured by images connected to their source code via automated builds. Docker Hub can automatically rebuild an image when its source code is updated on sites like GitHub or Bitbucket, keeping the image up to date with its codebase.

Docker Hub provides private repositories for businesses with specific privacy requirements. Private repositories are protected, accessible only by certain individuals or teams, whereas public repositories are available to the entire community. This functionality is significant for businesses or developers working with proprietary software because it protects their privacy of their Docker images.

Docker Hub is compatible with pipelines for continuous integration and deployment (CI/CD) that go beyond storage and retrieval. Build and deployment procedures are frequently automated in modern software development. After an image push, actions can be triggered via Docker Hub's webhooks and API connections. For example, a deployment tool may be immediately notified when a new image version is posted to Docker Hub, starting a rollout in a staging or production environment.

The importance of Docker Hub extends beyond its use by developers and companies; it is essential to the upbringing and education of the Docker community. Best practices, tutorials, and documentation are hosted on the platform. When someone is new to Docker, Docker Hub is frequently their first point of contact. It is where they may obtain official images, look through community contributions, and absorb the combined knowledge of seasoned Docker enthusiasts.

However, it's also important to take note of the advent of alternative registries in light of Docker Hub's growing significance. Some businesses choose to use third-party solutions or self-hosted registries because they require specific integrations or more control. Although Docker Hub is a dominant player in the registry market, the larger Docker ecosystem values diversity and has several registries to meet different demands.

In conclusion, Docker Hub will always have a significant role in the Docker world. It is a platform that combines storage, distribution, collaboration, and learning, linking users and image makers. Docker Hub is leading the way in the application development and deployment revolution as Docker continues to gain momentum, demonstrating the potential of containerization and the strength of community-driven innovation. In addition to facilitating software distribution, Docker Hub also reflects the values of sharing, trust, and international collaboration with each docker pull and push.

Building custom images using Dockerfile

The Dockerfile is a small but powerful tool that serves as the foundation of the entire Docker universe, where images are the main focus and containers are what make applications run. To fully utilize Docker's containerization, one must become proficient with the Dockerfile, just like a sculptor with his chisel. The bridge that connects uncompiled code to robust, portable containers has completely changed how software is developed and distributed. However, why is the Dockerfile so essential, and how does one create customized images with it? Together, we will explore the intricacies of Dockerfile and its essential function within the Docker paradigm.

A Dockerfile is a text script, a set of instructions that tells Docker how to build an image. Consider it like a recipe, where each line outlines a step that must be taken to create a food, in this case a Docker image. In contrast to traditional recipes, the Dockerfile is deterministic, meaning that the final image is always the same each time it is called. One of Docker's greatest accomplishments is its consistency, and the Dockerfile is fundamental to it.

The FROM directive is often the first line of a basic Dockerfile. This basic instruction represents the base image that will serve as the basis for the custom image. This might be a more general-purpose Linux distribution like Ubuntu or a lighter one like Alpine for a lot of applications. This foundation provides the fundamental OS layers that are built onto, allowing for installing other customizations.

After the foundation, a set of guidelines customizes the image to meet particular requirements. RUN is a commonly used command that instructs Docker to run commands in the image's environment. This could involve installing particular software packages or using apt-get update to update software repositories. Here is where the strength of the Dockerfile really shows off, enabling developers to automate the creation of the environment and guarantee that all dependencies and configurations are taken care of consistently.

However, what about the actual application code? How does it get into the image? Fortunately, the COPY and ADD commands are useful. Both allow files to be transferred from the host computer into the image but ADD also has the ability to handle URLs and do automatic archive extraction. Developers can therefore easily incorporate any necessary assets, configuration files, or source code for their application into the image.

Another strength of Dockerfile is setting the runtime behavior. When a container is started from the image, the commands that will be performed are defined by the CMD and ENTRYPOINT instructions. Both can establish default commands; however, CMD gives readily overridable defaults, while ENTRYPOINT offers a more rigid approach, making it the command the container will always execute. This distinction enables developers to create images that can default to particular behaviors or behave differently depending on input from the user.

In addition to these guidelines, Dockerfile provides environment-tuning tools. Setting environment variables, or key-value pairs that might affect how an application behaves, is done with the ENV command. Similarly, the WORKDIR instruction establishes the working directory inside the container and guarantees that any commands that follow run in this designated directory. Despite their subtlety, these instructions enable developers to design an environment specific to the requirements of their particular application.

But Dockerfile's layered architecture—rather than just its instructions—is what makes it so magical. After being processed, each Dockerfile directive adds a new layer to the image. The final image is created by stacking these layers on top of one another. This architectural strategy has significant ramifications. It promotes reusability, to start. Docker optimizes storage by reusing common layers shared by several images, hence conserving space. Second, Docker rebuilds only the layers from the point of change when a Dockerfile is modified, using cached layers for the previously unaltered phases. This guarantees effective storage management in addition to accelerating the production of images.

The process of producing the image is simple once the Dockerfile is written. When the docker build command is used, Docker reads the Dockerfile, follows each instruction one by one, and the result is a customized Docker image that is prepared for distribution or deployment.

In conclusion, despite its humble appearance, the Dockerfile transforms code and configurations into industry-standard Docker images. It is the alchemist's stone of the Docker universe. It reflects

Docker's values, which include consistency, automation, and portability. Understanding the Dockerfile is an art form for developers, not just a technical competency. It's the ability to design, produce, and distribute applications in a scalable, repeatable, and effective manner. The Dockerfile is proof positive that the most potent technologies often come in the simplest packages, especially as the world appreciates containerization.

Best practices for image creation

The production of Docker images takes on great significance in the realm of Docker, where consistency and portability are most promising. Docker image developers must follow best practices, just like professional painters who ensure every brushstroke adds to the final masterpiece. The complete application lifecycle, from development to production, can be significantly impacted by ensuring images are effective, safe, and customized for particular requirements. Now let's explore the various approaches to refine and elevate the Docker image building process to a fine art.

Minimalism is one of the core ideas behind creating Docker images. One can never overestimate the appeal of a simple, clutter-free look. It increases security by ensuring quicker deployment, less resource usage, and reducing the possible attack surface. The appropriate foundation image selection is essential to achieving this. Rather than using extensive, feature-rich OS images, consider using more basic ones, such as Alpine Linux. Only the necessary components are included in these images, leaving nothing else to make the program function. The 'less is more' mentality benefits Docker by guaranteeing that images are optimized for their intended use.

The layer optimization principle is a logical extension of minimalism. Each Dockerfile command adds a layer to the finished image. This layered architecture is likely to become bloated even if it offers advantages like caching and reusability. Developers should therefore be careful to keep the number of layers to a minimum. Layers can be efficiently reduced by combining instructions, particularly those that add files and subsequently alter them. For example, merging software installation and package repository updates into a single RUN command guarantees that both processes share a layer and create a smaller image than if done separately.

Another important component of the layered paradigm is order. Placing instructions that change frequently near the end of the Dockerfile guarantees that static layers are stored and reused during builds since Docker caches layers. This method guarantees effective bandwidth and storage use while expediting the image production process.

Security in the context of Docker cannot be an afterthought. Images need to be secure because they are the blueprint for containers. Updates to installed software packages and base images regularly guarantee that known security flaws are fixed. Additional security assurance can be obtained using tools like Docker's own 'Docker Scan' or third-party solutions like 'Trivy' to scan images for vulnerabilities. It's also a good idea to refrain from using containers to run processes as the root user. Potential risks are reduced by switching to a non-root user by using the USER instruction in the Dockerfile.

In the Docker ecosystem, traceability and transparency are virtues. Users and developers alike should have trust in the information included in an image. To that purpose, while choosing base images, give preference to official images or images from reliable sources. For example, official images that are verified and kept up to date by professionals are hosted on Docker Hub. When obtaining customized images from outside sources, make sure the sources are reliable and trustworthy. You should also think about checking the images for any irregularities.

Maintainability is a human factor that is sometimes overlooked in pursuing flawless images. Developers will read, update, and manage Dockerfiles just like they do any other code. It is easier to read and manage Dockerfiles if they are well-organized, consistently styled, and have well-commented sections. This method helps present developers and guarantees that subsequent partners will be able to comprehend and alter the image generation procedure easily.

Even though they are necessary, environment-specific setups can add variation to the process of creating images. You might want to use environment variables instead of building these into the image. The runtime flags may introduce these variables during container instantiation or by the ENV instruction in Dockerfiles. This guarantees that the image stays consistent, adding environmental variations only when needed.

Finally, despite the temptation to make manual adjustments and gain shell access to running containers, resist the desire. This method of altering containers makes any modifications transient and unreflected in the source image. Rather, make sure that any changes are always documented in the Dockerfile. This method ensures repeatability by ensuring the image is consistent with the developer's goal in each instantiation.

In conclusion, building Docker images is a sophisticated craft rather than a routine task. It strikes a balance between maintainability, security, and efficiency. Developers can make sure their Docker images are not only functional but also lightweight, safe, and consistent in the current software environment by following best practices. Applications are only as good as the containers they operate in in the quickly developing field of containerization, thus taking the time and making an effort to master image generation can pay off and increase the advantages Docker offers.

CHAPTER V

Managing Containers

Starting and stopping containers

Starting and stopping containers is like the heartbeat in the vast symphony of containerization, where Docker orchestrates a harmonic integration between programs and their environments. These seemingly straightforward operations exhibit a significant depth when examined through the prism of Docker's guiding principles. They include containerized workloads' transient nature, services orchestration, and applications' lifespan. Understanding the nuances of starting and stopping containers is essential to comprehend Docker completely. This will help to ensure applications launch successfully and terminate gracefully when their intended use is met.

The docker start command is the foundation of the Docker container lifecycle. However, a container needs to be made from an image, which acts as its blueprint, before it can be started. Using the docker create command, this creation process instantiates a container without executing it. On the other hand, developers typically use the docker run command—which combines creation and start actions—in real-world settings. Docker starts a container from the given image and launches it immediately when executed. Docker's instantaneous conversion from a static image to a dynamic container is a prime example of its portability and immediacy.

Starting a container takes more than just starting the main process specified in the image. It is an orchestra of setups, ranging from allocating resources to mounting volumes and specifying network connections to setting environment variables. The container's behavior is affected by each of these configurations, regardless of whether they are supplied as runtime arguments or described in the Dockerfile. For instance, certain environment variables that specify the login and password of a database container may be used when it is first started. Alternatively, a web server container may be started with port mappings enabled, allowing outside networks to access its services. Hence, the docker start procedure involves more than just starting an application; it also involves configuring the environment to meet the application's requirements and guaranteeing its smooth interaction with the larger ecosystem.

While stopping containers is an art of graceful termination, starting them is about creation and initiation. That's what the docker stop command does. Upon invocation, Docker requests that the container's main process terminate by sending it a SIGTERM signal. Docker intervenes with a SIGKILL signal to forcefully terminate the process if it doesn't exit after a grace period. By following this order, programs are guaranteed time to wind down, maybe freeing resources or saving state, before being permanently stopped.

Nevertheless, Docker has an even quicker way to end a command: docker kill. Bypassing the grace period, this command sends a SIGKILL signal straight away. Although useful, it is a sharp reminder of how transient containers are. Containers in the Docker world are frequently transient, existing for a while before disappearing. They don't have the same lifespan as conventional virtual machines. Rather, they uphold the concepts of disposability and immutability. When a container breaks down, it is stopped and replaced rather than fixed. This paradigm shift pushes developers toward distributed persistence and stateless architectures, significantly impacting application design.

It's critical to understand that containers are just temporary. Any data saved inside a container that is not on a mounted volume is lost when the container is stopped. The significance of external persistence mechanisms—whether they are traditional databases, cloud storage, or Docker volumes—is emphasized by this transient data lifecycle. Because of this, stopping a container serves as a checkpoint that upholds Docker's values of data durability and state management. Stopping a container is not only about terminating it.

Starting and stopping containers individually are important, but they become even more significant when considered together. Modern orchestration systems respond to application requests, failures, or upgrades by starting and stopping containers in bulk using mechanisms like Kubernetes or Docker Swarm. The importance of the container lifecycle is increased by these orchestration platforms, which guarantee applications' scalability, resilience, and evergreenness.

In conclusion, although fundamental, the actions of starting and stopping Docker containers serve as windows into the larger containerization concept. The transient nature of containerized workloads, graceful shutdown, fast deployment, and configurability are highlighted. Developers and operators must comprehend these lifecycles as they integrate their applications into the Docker environment. It guarantees that applications are up and running and thriving, meeting user needs, changing with the times, and maintaining their current state throughout lifecycles. Docker's heartbeat, which is the pulse of start and stop commands, is the heartbeat of contemporary, scalable, and robust applications.

Accessing logs and debugging

Logs are the silent recorders in the vast, complex software world, where services and applications are always coming and going. They record the whispers of procedures, the shouts of outliers, and the narratives of user exchanges. Logs are significant in the world of Docker, which is a universe unto itself where applications find a reliable, isolated shelter. They tell the story of containerized applications and serve as essential tools for developers and operators to solve puzzles, identify problems, and guarantee the best possible outcome for their deployments. Walking through the spaces of Docker's debugging tools and logging mechanisms, we discover a maze full of obstacles, opportunities, and answers.

Docker understands the importance of logs by design. Docker captures all of a container's standard error (STDERR) and standard output (STDOUT) streams while it is operating. This encapsulation makes sure that Docker is ready to listen and record, regardless of the many log production techniques that application may use, ranging from basic print statements to complex logging libraries. The docker logs command is the main way to retrieve these chronicles. Developers can access the complete verbal history of a container— from its initial echo to its most recent exclamation—with just one easy invocation. This simple process makes sure that their stories don't disappear into thin air, even in the face of container disposability and transience.

But Docker logs are more than just passive records—they can be actively controlled and redirected. Docker's adaptability in this field is demonstrated by its logging drivers. Docker supports various additional drivers, from cloud-based methods like AWS CloudWatch to centralized logging solutions like Fluentd or syslog. The default 'json-file' driver sends logs as local JSON files. Operators may make sure logs are sent to the right places—local storage for small deployments, or scalable, queryable platforms for large-scale operations—by configuring the right logging driver.

However, even with their great value, logs are the first step in troubleshooting. They frequently steer developers toward possible trouble spots by indicating symptoms. One may need to delve deeper to get a true diagnosis, particularly in a live setting. Docker offers a set of commands designed specifically for this use case. For example, the docker top command provides a snapshot of the processes that are executing within a container. One useful tool for a more interactive study is docker exec. It gives developers direct access to the file system, environment, and active services by enabling them to execute commands inside an active container. Despite its strength, this deep dive should only be used sparingly, always remembering the repeatability and immutability of the container.

Sometimes, the mysteries contained in containers are too complex for STDOUT and STDERR to explain. This is where Docker's compatibility with debugging tools shines. It is possible to put tools like gdb or strace inside of containers, giving developers more visibility and control. Furthermore, kernel-level debugging is now possible thanks to Docker's support for "privileged" containers with extra system capabilities. Although these instruments provide deep insights, they also can change the states of containers. It is therefore essential to employ them appropriately, maintaining container integrity and uniformity.

A crucial aspect of debugging that is frequently disregarded is monitoring. While logs record information in the past, real-time insights can be obtained by combining monitoring technologies such as Prometheus with visualization platforms like Grafana. Docker guarantees that these tools have a robust data source due to its metrics API and integration features. It is possible to monitor metrics such as CPU utilization, memory consumption, and network traffic, which gives developers a comprehensive understanding of the health of containers. Before problems appear in logs, anomalies in these measures may serve as early warning signs of problems.

However, the developer's perspective is frequently one of the most powerful tools in this extensive toolkit of logging and debugging techniques. Debugging can be turned from a reactive task to a proactive technique by adopting observability principles, which involve proactively instrumenting code using logging, metrics, and tracing. This proactive approach is not just good, but crucial in the world of Docker, where deployments are dynamic, repeatability is sacred, and applications are separated.

In conclusion, there is a science and an art to Docker logging and debugging. They combine analytical reasoning with technical tools, reactive approaches with proactive tactics. When applications move into Docker containers, developers and operators are responsible for ensuring that applications can communicate—their happy moments, sad moments, strange occurrences, and standard operating procedures. Logs, metrics, and debugging tools are some of the many channels of communication that Docker provides. By utilizing these, one may guarantee the seamless functioning of applications and the consistent, dependable, and scalable deployments in the constantly changing software landscape that Docker promises.

Persistent storage and volumes

There is a fascinating contradiction in the vast Docker ecosystem, where the environment is enclosed, and programs are containerized. Because of their very nature, containers are transient. They are created, fulfill their mission, and disappear into thin air. What about the data they generate and use, though? Data frequently outlives the applications that produce it, making preservation difficult, particularly in an environment where disposability is the norm. Discover the world of volumes and persistent storage with Docker— a confusing array of tactics, approaches, and tools that aim to balance the transient character of containers with the permanent quality of data.

Docker's primary goal is to separate dependent applications from the host system. Application code, runtime, libraries, and settings are all wrapped into a single, cohesive unit called a transient entity called a container. All data created within a container is, however, transient by design. The data that a container created vanishes along with it whenever it is removed or changed. This was a serious dilemma in the early days of containerization. How might the potential of containers be used to maintain the durability and accessibility of data?

Volumes were Docker's initial solution to this issue. Volumes are particularly specified folders meant to store data regardless of the container's lifecycle, and they work around the Union File System by default. Docker allocates a place on the host computer that the container can read from or write to when a developer establishes a volume. This implies that the data in the volume is unaffected even if the container is removed. Containers can share and reuse volumes, forming a bridge for data storage and interchange. To manage these permanent storage areas, use the docker volume command, which allows creating, deleting, listing, and examining volumes.

However, Docker went beyond just offering a persistence method. It increased the degree of control and flexibility. Volume mounts are one layer like this. Volume mounts let users mount any host directory into a container and have direct access to the host's file system, even though volumes are generated and maintained by Docker. This presents two benefits. Initially, it offers developers a simple way to input data or configuration files into containers. Since the data is stored directly on the host's file system, it provides a straightforward data migration and backup mechanism.

Nevertheless, more complex storage needs arose as Docker developed and gained popularity. Local volumes and mounts were insufficient in distributed multi-node deployments. Third-party storage platforms and network-attached storage solutions were necessary. Docker recognized this and released volume plugins, a mechanism that let outside companies sell storage solutions integrated with the volume system. This enabled products like NetApp, Amazon EBS, and DigitalOcean Block Storage to easily integrate with the Docker ecosystem and offer distributed, scalable storage alternatives that complemented Docker's native volumes.

Although volumes and related concepts tackled the issue of data durability, they also brought forth further difficulties, particularly concerning data portability. The world of Docker allows programs to be portable. On a developer's laptop, a program packaged into a container can operate in the same way on any Docker-compatible server. However, how could this portability be guaranteed, given that data is now anchored to volumes?

Volume drivers provided a solution for Docker. Docker stores volumes on the host's file system using the local driver by default. Nonetheless, various drivers, such as overlay2, aufs, or third-party plugins, are available for developers and operators to select from, each providing unique storage methods and advantages. Docker makes sure volumes are as portable as containers by using drivers to encapsulate the underlying storage mechanism, allowing volumes to be moved, backed up, or migrated without depending on a particular host or platform.

But in all of this complex persistence activity, one must remember that the applications themselves are the main consumers of these volumes. Applications have particular needs for consistency, data structures, and I/O patterns, particularly in the case of databases or file systems. Consequently, even though Docker offers persistence techniques, these mechanisms must match the applications' storage needs. Block storage, for example, could be advantageous for a database since it guarantees quick, low-latency data access. On the other hand, a file-sharing program might be more inclined toward object storage since it values scalability and metadata.

In conclusion, Docker's tale of volumes and persistent storage is one of development, difficulties, and resolutions. It emphasizes Docker's dedication to offering applications a comprehensive environment where data persists gracefully, and code operates without interruptions. For developers and operators, the interactions between volumes, volume mounts, drivers, and plugins create many possibilities. But it requires knowledge and careful application, just like any other strong tool. Applications and their persistent data are having an increasingly important dialogue as they get closer to a containerized future. Docker guarantees that this conversation is not only continued but also expanded through its storage solutions, implying a time when data is eternal while applications are transient.

Networking and linking containers

Isolation and interaction are in continual conflict in the huge world of Docker, where applications thrive in the warm embrace of containers. Applications are encapsulated within Docker containers by design, providing a consistent environment free from outside disruptions. However, applications are rarely isolated like any other entity in the contemporary software ecosystem. They communicate, work together, and occasionally conflict. Docker dives deeply into networking and linking, a field where the physics of connectedness intersects with the poetry of isolation, to enable these complex interactions while preserving their sanctum of isolation.

The voyage starts with a seemingly straightforward inquiry: how can a container communicate with the outside world? Docker was initially developed with the idea of simplicity as its foundation. Each container would be assigned A private IP address, keeping it hidden from the host and other containers. This was accomplished by connecting containers to a private bridge on the host via virtual Ethernet pairs, which functioned as conduits over the native Linux networking stack. The outside world could interact with the container through port mappings, which include tunneling particular host ports to the container's ports. The 'bridge networking' method ensured containers could communicate with the outside world while granting them network independence.

But as use-cases and Docker gained traction, it became obvious that a one-size-fits-all approach to networking was not the best one. In some instances, containers have to communicate with the host openly or even completely avoid using the host's networking stack. Docker introduces "none networking," in which a container has its own network namespace but no access to external networks, and "host networking," in which a container shares the host's network namespace, to handle this multitude of demands. These modes provided operators and developers with fine-grained control over container networking, enabling them to match connection plans to specific application needs.

However, the true difficulty was in getting containers to communicate with one another rather than with the outside world. Applications in the microservices-driven world are frequently a patchwork of interconnected services, each operating in a separate container and requiring different networking. 'Linking' was Docker's first solution to this challenge. Developers could establish a secure communication between containers by starting a container with the --link flag. Sharing environment variables and establishing a network connection made it possible for containers to find and interact with one another without any problems. Linking was revolutionary when it came to providing a straightforward method of inter-container communication without exposing them to outside networks.

However, because software is a constantly changing field, Docker's networking difficulties became more intricate. Although elegant, linking was static. It was not designed to accommodate the dynamic nature of modern deployments, where containers are created and destroyed regularly, and it required explicit declarations at container start-up. A dynamic, adaptable, and scalable networking solution was in high demand.

In response, Docker unveiled its networking technology, which would act as the foundation for connectivity between containers and be extensible and pluggable. Its core component was the "network driver," a plugin-based framework that allowed various networking techniques to be used in accordance with use cases. The 'overlay' driver, which enables multi-host networking for distributed applications, and the 'macvlan' driver, which permits containers to be directly allocated MAC addresses, were alternatives available to developers in addition to the default 'bridge' driver, which preserved the conventional bridge networking methodology.

Nevertheless, the "user-defined bridge network" was arguably the pinnacle of Docker's novel networking paradigm. User-defined bridges provided automatic DNS resolution for container names, which made service discovery easier than with the default bridge network. With the use of simple service names, containers may now locate and interact with one another without the requirement for common environment variables or explicit linkages.

Docker Compose, a tool that gave multi-container applications orchestration capabilities, complemented this new networking paradigm. Developers could provide network configurations, service dependencies, and other details for a multi-service application in a single file using Compose. Compose would ensure services were linked to the right networks when launched, honoring dependencies and guaranteeing smooth communication. When apps were running across many containers, Compose took on the role of conductor, arranging the connectivity symphony.

In conclusion, Docker's experience in networking and linking is evidence of its dedication to change, advance, and innovate. Docker has worked tirelessly to balance the competing demands of isolation and interaction, starting with the simple days of bridge networking and progressing to the intricate movement of network drivers and user-defined bridges. The limitations of monolithic applications will give way to microservices applications, which will present increasing connectivity problems. In addition to ensuring connectivity, Docker's networking solutions guarantee scalable, secure, and effective interactions. Docker ensures that in the immense universe of software, where services are the stars and applications are the constellations, they always shine together, never colliding.

CHAPTER IV

Docker Compose:
Orchestrating Multi-container Applications

Basics of Docker Compose

Docker has significantly impacted how we view and manage application environments in the ethereal symphony of software development. With its birth, monolithic architectures gave way to microservice-driven ones, in which every service lives inside a container and executes its function with unmatched consistency. But this change also brought a new challenge: how can one keep track of the growing number of containers while ensuring they all work together, are set up properly, and don't lose their transient nature? This is where Docker Compose shines: a master conducting the orchestra of containers and guaranteeing that each note is played precisely.

Understanding the complexity that Docker Compose aims to manage is necessary before one can fully appreciate it. Many containers, including web servers, databases, cache layers, and more, may be included in a modern application, all of which are intricately entwined in a delicate web of dependencies. It becomes a jigsaw puzzle of setups and commands to initialize each container with the correct parameters, make sure they connect on the relevant network ports, and handle data persistence. Handling these components by hand becomes tedious and prone to mistakes, which can cause discrepancies across the environments used for development, testing, and production. This complex web has an answer in the form of Docker Compose, which provides a declarative, simplified method for creating and maintaining multi-container Docker applications.

The docker-compose.yml file, a YAML-formatted file that lists an application's services, networks, and volumes, is the central component of Docker Compose. This file is where the magic starts. Every service is represented by a container created from an image, which may be a customized Dockerfile-built image or one already pre-built. Developers have the ability to designate the networks that the container should connect to, the ports that should be opened, the environment variables that should be injected, and even the context in which the image should be constructed. This fine-grained degree of control, expressed understandably, guarantees that initializing and configuring containers is now a systematic, documented procedure rather than a confusing jumble of commands.

Docker Compose provides tools to specify inter-service dependencies beyond the individual services. Developers can control the sequence in which services are built and started by utilizing the depends_on attribute. This allows them to make sure that a database, for example, is properly setup before a web service that depends on it boots up. This degree of orchestration is essential in a microservices environment because it guarantees that services are synchronized in their interactions and segregated in their operations.

Another area where Docker Compose excels is in network management. Within the Docker ecosystem, networks function as channels for communication between containers. Although Docker comes with default networks, there are situations in which custom networks—which require specific drivers and configurations—are essential. Developers can specify these networks using Docker Compose in the docker-compose.yml file, which guarantees that services are connected in accordance with the architectural requirements of the application. Additionally, services can connect through service names by leveraging the DNS-based service discovery provided by user-defined networks; this feature makes settings easier to understand and improves readability.

Another essential component of application designs, data persistence and management, is also included in Docker Compose. The Compose file is where volumes, Docker's persistent storage solution, are defined and managed. Docker Compose allows you to handle data precisely, whether it's binding a host directory to a container path or employing named volumes that last longer than container lifecycles.

Nevertheless, Docker Compose handles the lifetime management of applications in addition to their definition. Developers may easily launch an entire application stack with the docker-compose up command or gracefully shut it down with the docker-compose down command when using the docker-compose command-line tool. With the ability to start, stop, build, and view individual services, a high degree of control over the application environment is provided. This feature and the Compose file's declarative structure guarantee environments' portability, consistency, and reproducibility. The application structure doesn't change whether a developer is working locally or deploying to a test environment, which lessens the "it works on my machine" mentality.

In conclusion, Docker Compose perfectly captures the spirit of Docker: reducing complexity, optimizing workflows, and guaranteeing consistency. There's no denying the necessity of a conductor as the range of services grows and applications get more complicated. Docker Compose acts as that conductor, directing the orchestra of containers toward a harmonious performance using its declarative approach, orchestration features, and lifecycle management tools. Docker Compose is a monument to the strength of automation, abstraction, and simplicity in a world where the lines between development and operations are blurring and agility is critical.

Writing a docker-compose.yml file

Docker has become an efficient and consistent light in the large field of software development. Developers embraced the paradigm shift that allowed them to encapsulate applications within containers as the Docker tool suite grew and matured. But when microservices and multi-container architectures increased, a new difficulty emerged: coordinating the harmonious movement of several containers. Docker Compose elegantly responded to this need by offering a smooth method for defining and controlling applications with multiple containers. The docker-compose.yml file, which describes an application's services, interactions, and organizational structure, is essential to this functionality.

The docker-compose.yml file represents more than just a configuration; it encapsulates the essence of an application's architecture. Writing this file is akin to crafting a musical score, where each service is an instrument, and the networks and volumes are the harmonies that bind them together. As we delve into the art of writing this file, it becomes clear that mastering its nuances allows developers to breathe life into their applications, ensuring every container plays its part to perfection.

Determining the Docker Compose file format version is the initial step in this process. Docker Compose has seen numerous iterations as with any evolving software, with each version bringing new capabilities and improvements. By specifying the version at the beginning of the file, developers ensure that the subsequent definitions adhere to the syntax and semantics of that particular iteration. It's a contract of sorts, ensuring that the tools and the definitions speak the same language.

With the version set, the stage is ready for the main actors—the services. Each service in the docker-compose.yml file corresponds to a containerized application or component. It's within the service definitions that the magic begins to unfold. Every service is sourced from an image—a snapshot encapsulating the application and its environment. This image could be a pre-built one from Docker Hub or other registries or could be built from a custom Dockerfile, tailoring the environment to the application's needs. By specifying the build context or the image name, developers lay the foundation for the service.

But a service is more than just its image. It thrives on configurations—environment variables that tailor its behavior, ports that expose its interfaces, and networks that determine its interactions. Within the service definition, developers can articulate these aspects with precision. Ports can be mapped from the host to the container, ensuring accessibility. Environment variables, either hard-coded or sourced from external files, breathe life into the applications, providing the necessary context for their execution.

However, services in a microservices architecture seldom operate in isolation. They interact, depend on each other, and sometimes need to be orchestrated in a specific sequence. Docker Compose offers tools to capture these intricacies. By leveraging constructs like depends_on, developers can define the order of service initialization, ensuring, for instance, that a database is ready before a web server trying to connect to it is started. Similarly, links and networks allow for the creation of communication channels between services, ensuring they can discover and interact with each other in a structured manner.

Beyond services, the docker-compose.yml file also provides constructs for defining networks and volumes—two pillars supporting the services' edifice. In the Docker universe, networks are the highways along which services communicate. While Docker provides default networks, there are scenarios where custom configurations or isolated networks are essential. The network definition section in the Compose file allows for creating these custom networks, complete with specific drivers and configurations. Volumes, on the other hand, are the keepers of data, ensuring that stateful information persists beyond the transient life of containers. Whether binding specific host directories to container paths or creating named volumes that outlive container lifecycles, Docker Compose offers the tools to manage data with nuance and precision.

Writing the docker-compose.yml file is an exercise in clarity, foresight, and understanding. It requires developers to visualize their application's architecture, understand the interplay of services, and foresee potential interaction pitfalls. But the rewards of this exercise are manifold. With a well-crafted Compose file, bringing an application to life is as simple as invoking docker-compose up. Every service starts in its designated order; every configuration is applied, and the application hums to life, just as envisioned.

In conclusion, a Dockerized multi-container application's docker-compose.yml file is its brain. It serves as a narrative, a guide, and a plan all at once. Developers who become experts at producing this file will guarantee consistency, reproducibility, and harmony in their applications in addition to streamlining their workflows. The docker-compose.yml file is the conductor of the orchestra of containers in the grand concert of software development, leading them to a perfect performance.

Scaling with Docker Compose

When the container era emerged, it showed developers the way toward isolation, consistency, and portability. Docker is a program that began life as a primary platform for containerization but quickly developed to meet the ever-growing demands of the software industry. One such development was Docker Compose, an advantage to developers who had long yearned for a simple means of coordinating the movements of numerous containers. Although the ability to define, manage, and execute multi-container Docker applications was a significant advancement, scaling services revealed another side to this elegance. With Docker Compose, scaling—which is frequently a challenging process full of architectural and infrastructure difficulties—became amazingly easier. This section explores the science and art of scaling using Docker Compose, demonstrating how it can revolutionize software deployment and administration.

In the lexicon of software engineering, scaling is the ability of an application or system to handle increased loads effectively. As user bases grow and demands surge, systems are expected to perform consistently, often requiring increased resources or instances of services. Historically, scaling operations, whether horizontal (adding more instances) or vertical (adding more resources), were significant endeavors, involving detailed planning, configuration, and often substantial downtime. The beauty of Docker Compose lies in its ability to simplify this intricate process, turning what was once a Herculean task into a series of straightforward commands.

At the heart of Docker Compose's scaling capabilities is its service-centric architecture. Each service, defined within the docker-compose.yml file, corresponds to a containerized application component. When conceived, Docker Compose services typically represented single instances of these components. However, as the need for scalability became evident, Docker Compose adapted, allowing multiple instances of these services to be easily orchestrated. This inherent adaptability transformed Docker Compose from a tool that could orchestrate complex applications to one that could scale them effortlessly.

The mechanics of scaling with Docker Compose are elegantly simple. Utilizing the docker-compose up --scale command, developers can specify which service they intend to scale and to what extent. For example, if one has a web service defined within the Compose file and wishes to scale it to three instances, it's as uncomplicated as invoking docker-compose up --scale web=3. Behind the scenes, Docker Compose manages the intricacies—creating the necessary containers, ensuring they adhere to the defined configurations, and orchestrating their startup. This process, which might have involved substantial manual intervention in traditional architectures, becomes almost instantaneous.

However, the beauty of Docker Compose's scaling capabilities isn't just in the act itself but in the seamless integration with other features. As services scale, their networking needs grow. Containers must communicate, discover each other, and sometimes even load-balance requests. Docker Compose's inherent networking capabilities shine in this context. As services scale, each instance (or container) retains the service's network configurations. If a custom network was defined, each instance would automatically join it, benefiting from Docker's built-in DNS for service discovery. This ensures that even as services expand, they remain interconnected and capable of communicating without additional configurations.

But scaling services isn't without its challenges. One of the primary considerations is state management, especially for stateful services like databases. While stateless services (like stateless web servers) can be scaled without much forethought about individual instance states, stateful services require a more nuanced approach. Docker Compose, while primarily a tool for orchestrating containers, doesn't inherently solve stateful scaling problems but provides the tools (like volumes) to manage persistent data. When scaling stateful services, external tools or patterns, such as sharding or replication, often play a significant role.

Another subtle aspect of scaling with Docker Compose is ensuring idempotency. The system's overall state should remain consistent as services scale up or down. Docker Compose ensures this by making scaling operations idempotent. If a service is scaled to five instances and a subsequent command attempts to scale it to five again, Docker Compose recognizes the state and doesn't redundantly recreate containers. This level of intelligence ensures that scaling operations are efficient and minimizes potential disruptions.

In conclusion, Docker Compose's capacity to expand services is evidence of its development and reflects the dynamic requirements of contemporary applications. What formerly needed careful planning, substantial resource allocation, and complex execution has been reduced to a set of straightforward instructions. The infrastructure requirements of applications change as they get larger, and Docker Compose is prepared to handle these changes, transforming the difficulties of scaling into a symphony of planned expansion. Docker Compose stands out as a beacon of light in the wide world of software development and deployment, pointing developers in the direction of scalability in an elegant and straightforward manner.

CHAPTER VII

Streamlining Development with Docker

Setting up a development environment using Docker

In the rich tapestry of software development, few challenges have been as perennial as environment inconsistencies. The phrase, "It works on my machine," has been an oft-repeated refrain, symptomatic of discrepancies between development, staging, and production environments. For developers, these inconsistencies can be both a source of frustration and a significant drain on productivity. However, as the cloud of these challenges loomed large, a silver lining emerged in the form of Docker—a tool that promised and delivered consistency, portability, and efficiency. Docker's value proposition, while impactful in production, truly shines in development environments, offering developers a canvas to craft, test, and iterate applications with unprecedented ease. This section delves into the transformative journey of setting up a development environment using Docker, shedding light on its nuances, benefits, and overarching impact on the software development lifecycle.

Establishing a Docker-based development environment begins with understanding Docker's foundational promise: containerization. At its core, containerization is about encapsulation. Applications, with all their dependencies, configurations, and runtime requirements, are bundled into containers—lightweight, isolated, and consistent software units. By being detached from the underlying host system, these containers ensure uniformity across varied environments. When a developer encapsulates their application within a Docker container, they're not just packaging software; they're creating an ecosystem—a miniaturized, controlled environment where the application operates precisely as intended, regardless of where the container is run.

With this foundational knowledge, the next step is to tailor Docker for development. The first consideration is creating a Docker image—the blueprint from which containers are instantiated. For developers, this image is more than just a static snapshot; it's a dynamic entity evolving with the application's needs. Crafting this image involves writing a Dockerfile—a declarative script that outlines the base OS, dependencies, software installations, and configurations. In a development context, this Dockerfile often leans towards verbosity, ensuring that debugging tools, development libraries, and other ancillary software are included. This results in an environment that, while bulkier than a production setup, offers developers a rich toolkit to craft and refine applications.

Having defined the environment's blueprint, developers can use Docker to bring it to life. The Dockerfile is transformed into an image and subsequently a running container using commands like docker build and docker run. The application finds a home within this container—a consistent, isolated, and controlled space where it operates, unaffected by host-specific quirks or external inconsistencies. Developers can interact with this container, much like a local development server, but with the added assurance of consistency.

One of Docker's standout features in a development context is its ability to mount volumes. While containers are inherently ephemeral, development often requires persistence for databases, application logs, or other stateful data. Docker volumes address this need, allowing developers to bind specific directories on the host system to paths within the container. This ensures that data persists across container lifecycles, facilitating iterative development without data loss.

Beyond individual applications, modern software development often involves orchestrating multiple services—databases, caches, microservices, and more. Docker Compose, a tool within the Docker ecosystem, shines in this context. Developers can use a docker-compose.yml file to define multi-container applications, specifying inter-service dependencies, network configurations, and shared volumes. With a single docker-compose up command, this intricate orchestra comes to life, with each service playing its part in harmony.

However, the beauty of Docker in development isn't just in its foundational capabilities but in its ecosystem. The Docker Hub, a repository of pre-built images, offers developers a head start. Whether one needs a specific version of a database, a particular configuration of a web server, or a pre-tailored development environment, the Docker Hub likely has an image that fits the bill. This, combined with Docker's layering system, ensures that developers can bootstrap environments rapidly, building upon the community's collective knowledge.

While Docker's benefits in development environments are manifold, it's also essential to recognize its learning curve. Docker introduces a paradigm shift, and developers, especially those unfamiliar with containerization, might face initial hurdles. However, these challenges are transient. As one delves deeper into Docker, its elegance becomes evident, turning initial hurdles into long-term efficiencies.

In conclusion, Docker's impact on development environments is transformative. It addresses a long-standing challenge, turning the dream of consistent, portable, and efficient environments into a tangible reality. By encapsulating applications, abstracting away host-specific inconsistencies, and offering tools to manage complex orchestrations, Docker empowers developers to focus on what truly matters—crafting exceptional software. In the grand narrative of software development, Docker emerges as a tool and a philosophy emphasizing the importance of consistency, collaboration, and efficiency.

Using Docker in Continuous Integration/Continuous Deployment (CI/CD)

In the modern panorama of software development, the rhythm and pace of releases have undergone a dramatic transformation. Gone are the days of monolithic releases that saw the light of day after long, grueling months of development and testing. Today, the software world dances to the tune of Continuous Integration and Continuous Deployment - a symphony of consistent code integrations, automated tests, and frequent, reliable deployments. At the heart of this evolution, ensuring its fluidity and elegance, stands Docker, a tool that embodies consistency, isolation, and portability. This section explores the intricate ballet of using Docker in CI/CD, exploring its nuances, advantages, and transformative influence on the software delivery lifecycle.

At its essence, CI/CD represents a paradigm shift in how software is developed, tested, and deployed. Continuous Integration emphasizes regularly merging code changes into a central repository, followed by automated tests to ensure consistency and quality. Continuous Deployment takes this a step further, automating the deployment process, ensuring that code changes, once tested, are automatically deployed to production or staging environments. The overarching goal is clear: reduce manual intervention, minimize errors, and accelerate delivery. However, as noble as these objectives are, their realization is fraught with challenges. Enter Docker, a beacon of consistency in the turbulent seas of software development.

The harmony between Docker and CI/CD begins with the very principles that Docker champions: containerization. Every stage in the CI/CD pipeline, from integration to testing to deployment, requires a consistent environment. Variabilities in system configurations, software versions, or dependencies introduce uncertainties that undermine the CI/CD promise. With their encapsulated, consistent, and isolated nature, Docker containers address this challenge head-on. Docker removes the infamous "it works on my machine" dilemma from the CI/CD equation by ensuring that applications and their environments are bundled into uniform units. Every stage of the pipeline, whether running unit tests, integration tests, or deployment scripts, operates on the exact environment the application was designed to run, ensuring consistency from development to production.

For Continuous Integration, in particular, Docker's value proposition is multi-fold. As developers merge code changes, CI servers like Jenkins, Travis CI, or GitLab CI spring into action, pulling the latest code and initiating a series of tests. Docker's lightweight nature ensures that fresh containers can be spun up rapidly for every integration, ensuring that tests run in pristine, controlled environments. Whether it's a specific database version for integration tests or a particular configuration of a web server for end-to-end tests, Docker ensures that CI servers have precisely what they need. Furthermore, Docker's ability to layer images means that CI servers can cache base images, reducing build and setup times and accelerating the feedback loop to developers.

The dance proceeds to Continuous Deployment, and Docker's elegance shines even brighter. Deployment, historically a complex process involving intricate configurations, environment setups, and manual interventions, has become significantly streamlined with Docker. CD tools can pull pre-configured Docker images, ensuring that the deployment environment, whether staging or production, mirrors the development and testing setups. The transient nature of containers ensures that deployments are clean, with every release getting a fresh environment, free from legacy configurations or lingering data. Moreover, with tools like Docker Compose, multi-container applications with interdependencies can be deployed with a single command, ensuring that the orchestration of complex applications is smooth and error-free.

However, Docker's role in CI/CD isn't just as a passive player ensuring environment consistency. Docker has actively shaped the CI/CD ecosystem, with emerging tools and platforms built on Docker's principles. Solutions like Google's Kubernetes, a container orchestration platform, have redefined how deployments are managed, scaled, and monitored, with Docker containers being the fundamental unit of deployment.

Yet, as with any transformative tool, integrating Docker into CI/CD comes with its considerations. An inherent learning curve requires teams to understand Docker's paradigms, craft optimized Dockerfiles, and manage image repositories. Security, too, comes into focus, especially when deploying containers to production. Ensuring that Docker images are free from vulnerabilities, regularly updated, and sourced from trusted repositories becomes paramount.

In conclusion, Docker's influence on the CI/CD landscape is profound, bridging the gap between development and operations, ensuring that the pipeline from code to deployment is smooth, consistent, and rapid. It addresses some of the most significant challenges in CI/CD, turning potential pain points into seamless processes. In the orchestra of software delivery, Docker plays a pivotal role, harmonizing tools, processes, and teams, ensuring that the music of rapid, reliable software releases never misses a beat.

Hot-reloading and efficient local development

In the grand composition of software development, efficiency and responsiveness play lead roles. The rhythm of writing code, testing changes, and seeing results should be as uninterrupted as possible, akin to a continuous melody. Traditionally, any disruption in this flow, like manually rebuilding environments or restarting applications, was akin to a discordant note, jarring and counterproductive. With its container-centric approach to application management, Docker ushered in the capability for hot-reloading, a feature that, like a masterful conductor, ensures that the development of music never stops. This section delves into the magic of hot-reloading within Docker and how it revolutionizes local development, offering a seamless, efficient, and interactive experience.

Imagine a painter constantly stepping back after each brushstroke, waiting for the paint to dry before assessing the impact of their action. This stop-and-start approach would hinder creativity and prolong the creation process. Similarly, the ability to write code and instantaneously witness its behavior is pivotal in software development. Hot-reloading, in essence, is the realization of this immediacy. It eliminates the need for unmanageable restarts or rebuilds and allows developers to make modifications to their code and see the results instantly. But what makes this possible in the realm of Docker, and how does it elevate local development to a new zenith of efficiency?

At its core, Docker is about encapsulating applications and their dependencies into isolated containers. However, the magic of Docker doesn't stop at merely isolating applications. It extends its capabilities to bridge the containerized environment with the local development environment. This bridge is facilitated through the use of 'volume mounts' in Docker. When setting up a container, developers can bind a local directory (which may contain the application's source code) to a directory within the container. This binding creates a real-time link between the two environments. Any changes made locally are instantaneously reflected within the container and vice versa.

Integrating this volume-based synchronization with tools and frameworks that support hot-reloading creates an environment where code changes are immediately mirrored inside the running container and, consequently, the running application picks up these changes and reloads itself. Consider web development frameworks like React or Vue.js. These frameworks come with built-in hot-reloading capabilities. When they run inside a Docker container set up with appropriate volume mounts, developers can edit their components, styles, or scripts locally, and the web application inside the Docker container updates in real-time, reflecting these changes without a full-page reload.

The implications of this are profound. Firstly, developers maintain their flow state. Cognitive science has repeatedly highlighted the benefits of uninterrupted focus, and with hot-reloading, the context-switching overheads—moving from coding to testing—are minimized. Developers remain in their zone, leading to heightened productivity and, often, better code quality.

Secondly, hot-reloading within Docker retains the benefits of containerization. Even as developers enjoy a fluid development experience, the application still runs in a controlled, consistent environment that mirrors production setups. This ensures that while the feedback loop is immediate, it's also accurate. Developers can be confident that the behavior they observe locally will match the behavior in other environments, reducing the notorious "works on my machine" syndrome.

Moreover, this efficiency extends to debugging as well. With real-time synchronization between local and containerized environments, tools that rely on source maps or other debug information can function seamlessly. Developers can make a code change, set breakpoints, and interactively debug, all while the application runs inside the container.

However, while hot-reloading in Docker amplifies local development efficiency, it's not without its caveats. Implementing hot-reloading necessitates a nuanced understanding of Docker volumes, file synchronization, and the intricacies of the development frameworks in use. Bidirectional synchronization carries the risk of "polluting" the local development environment if it is not handled appropriately. For instance, some processes might generate logs or temporary files that, if not managed, could spill over to the local environment.

Furthermore, developers must remain aware of performance implications. File synchronization between local systems and Docker containers, especially in large codebases or when using certain types of file systems, can introduce latency. Optimizing volume mounts, selectively synchronizing necessary directories, and occasionally tweaking native file system events can help mitigate these challenges.

In conclusion, hot-reloading in Docker has ushered in a new era of local development efficiency. It represents a harmonious blend of immediate feedback and consistent environments, ensuring developers can code with rhythm, focus, and confidence. As with any powerful tool, its effective use demands understanding, discretion, and occasional fine-tuning. Yet, when orchestrated well, hot-reloading in Docker transforms local development from a disjointed series of tasks into a flowing symphony of creation, iteration, and refinement.

CHAPTER VIII

Docker Swarm and Kubernetes:
An Introduction to Orchestration

Scaling applications with Docker Swarm

In the vast and complex world of distributed systems, ensuring the scalability and reliability of applications is paramount. As technology evolves and user bases grow, the ability of applications to seamlessly handle increasing loads without faltering becomes critical. Traditional scaling approaches, often manual and labor-intensive, can't always meet modern demands. With its containerization prowess, Docker brought about an elegant solution to this challenge. Among Docker's suite of tools, Docker Swarm emerges as a front-runner in orchestrating containers, making scaling feasible and fluid. This section delves deep into the realm of Docker Swarm, elucidating how it serves as a cornerstone for scaling applications with finesse and agility.

At its essence, Docker Swarm is Docker's native container orchestration tool. While containerization with Docker encapsulates applications, Docker Swarm takes it a step further by managing and orchestrating these containers across multiple machines. It's similar to a maestro who knows every instrument and understands how to bring them together to create a harmonious symphony. With Docker Swarm, containers are not isolated entities but part of a coordinated cluster, working in tandem to ensure the application's high availability and scalability.

When one begins their journey with Docker Swarm, they're introduced to the concept of 'nodes.' A node is any machine, be it physical or virtual, that runs an instance of the Docker daemon and is part of the swarm. There are two types of nodes, the 'Manager' and 'Worker'. While both can run containers, the Manager node shoulders the additional responsibility of orchestrating and scheduling containers across the cluster. The Worker node, true to its name, simply executes the containers as instructed by the Manager. This separation ensures efficient delegation and adds a layer of security, as worker nodes don't need complete access to the swarm's internal machinations.

The next piece in the Docker Swarm puzzle is the 'service.' In the swarm lingo, a service represents a task or a set of tasks, which could be running specific containers with specific images. When declaring a service in a swarm, you specify which container image to employ and which commands to execute inside those containers. But Docker Swarm truly shines in its ability to declare the desired state of services. For instance, if you dictate that a service should always have ten container instances running, Docker Swarm maintains this state. If a container fails, another is spun up automatically to keep the desired number.

As the application grows and user demands surge, how does Docker Swarm facilitate scaling? The answer lies in its 'replica' feature. Simply by updating the service's replica count, one can either increase or decrease the number of container instances for that service. Imagine an e-commerce platform experiencing heightened traffic during a sale. Instead of deploying more servers or manually starting more containers, with Docker Swarm, scaling becomes as simple as updating a number. As the swarm receives this updated desired state, it springs into action, distributing and starting containers across the nodes in the cluster, ensuring optimal load distribution and resource utilization.

But Docker Swarm doesn't stop at merely starting or stopping containers. It integrates deeply with Docker's networking capabilities to ensure these containers can communicate with each other and the outside world. Whether a service-to-service communication within the swarm or an external application accessing a service inside the swarm, Docker Swarm's in-built DNS ensures smooth networking. This ensures that services remain interconnected, aware, and cohesive as services scale.

However, like any powerful system, Docker Swarm has its challenges. First, while Docker Swarm excels in its simplicity and ease of use, especially when compared to other orchestrators like Kubernetes, it might not offer the granular control or extensive feature set that complex, enterprise-scale applications might demand. Second, given its distributed nature, understanding and troubleshooting network issues within a swarm can sometimes be daunting. Finally, maintaining a state across scalable, distributed applications—especially databases—requires careful consideration, as not all applications or databases are inherently designed for such scalability.

Yet, despite these challenges, Docker Swarm stands as a testament to the evolution of application scaling. Gone are the days of manual deployments, frantic server provisioning, or midnight outages due to load spikes. With Docker Swarm, applications are not only scalable but are resilient, self-healing, and adaptable. The paradigm has shifted from reacting to demands to proactively preparing for them.

In conclusion, Docker Swarm paints a future where applications gracefully scale with demands, minimize downtimes, and optimize resource utilization. It embodies the principles of modern application development: agility, scalability, and reliability. As businesses and developers tread further into this distributed future, tools like Docker Swarm will be their compass, guiding them through challenges and ensuring their applications remain robust and responsive, come what may.

Introduction to Kubernetes

In the vast digital ocean where applications form the islands of functionality and data rivers flow with intensity, the need to orchestrate, manage, and navigate becomes paramount. Just as the captain and crew navigate a ship through challenging waters, ensuring its course is suitable and responding to the changing environment, modern applications, primarily containerized ones, require a similar steering mechanism. Introducing Kubernetes, fondly termed K8s, the helmsman of the container world, ensuring that our digital ships not only stay afloat but sail with precision and agility.

Kubernetes traces its origins back to Google, which, after years of running production workloads at scale with its internal system Borg, decided to release Kubernetes as an open-source project in 2014. Kubernetes, which means "helmsman" or "pilot" in Greek, is a suitable name for its container orchestration function. Basically, Kubernetes is a framework for container orchestration that makes automating the deployment, scaling, and management of containerized applications possible. In a world where flexibility, scalability, and resilience are the gold standards of software design, Kubernetes emerges as the essential tool to achieve these goals.

The underlying philosophy of Kubernetes is declarative configuration and automation. Instead of manually pushing containers onto servers or setting up networking configurations, one simply declares the desired state for their application using a set of configurations. Kubernetes then takes up the mantle of ensuring the system matches this desired state. If a container fails, Kubernetes knows to replace it. If network traffic surges, Kubernetes can load balance the demand. Essentially, it's like setting the destination on a ship's autopilot and letting the system navigate, adjusting to the currents, winds, and obstacles.

At the heart of Kubernetes lies its architecture, which, though intricate, provides the scaffolding on which the vast capabilities of the platform are built. The Kubernetes cluster is the fundamental operational unit, and a series of nodes are within this cluster. The

Master node, often considered the brain of the Kubernetes operations, is responsible for maintaining the cluster's desired state. It makes the critical decisions about which containers run on which nodes, handling the scheduling intricacies. As the name suggests, the Worker nodes are where the containers (grouped in 'pods') run. These nodes are the foot soldiers, doing the heavy lifting while continuously communicating with the Master node.

One of the standout features of Kubernetes is its abstraction of the container in the form of 'pods.' While containers house the application, Kubernetes uses pods as the smallest deployable units that can be created, scheduled, and managed. A pod can host multiple containers that form a single unit of deployment. This design ensures that containers within a pod can easily communicate and share the same local network.

However, what truly amplifies Kubernetes' prowess is its suite of powerful functionalities that cater to almost every need of a modern containerized application. Services in Kubernetes provide stable endpoints for pods, abstracting away the dynamism associated with pod lifecycle, ensuring smooth network communication. Persistent storage, a critical aspect of stateful applications, is handled via Persistent Volumes (PVs) and Persistent Volume Claims (PVCs), abstracting the underlying storage backend. Then there's the powerful Horizontal Pod Autoscaler, which automatically scales the number of pods in response to CPU utilization or other select metrics. It's akin to the ship automatically adjusting its sails based on the wind intensity.

Yet, Kubernetes is not just about the technical nitty-gritty. It represents a paradigm shift in software development, deployment, and maintenance. The traditional challenges associated with environment discrepancies, scaling bottlenecks, and manual interventions are alleviated with Kubernetes. Developers can focus on crafting their applications, knowing that once handed over to Kubernetes, the intricacies of deployment and scaling are handled. Operations teams find solace in the platform's ability to self-heal, manage resources, and ensure high availability.

However, Kubernetes, with all its brilliance, isn't without its challenges. The sheer depth of its functionality means that its learning curve is steep. Configurations can be intricate, and understanding the interactions between various Kubernetes objects requires time and experience. Moreover, while Kubernetes abstracts away much of the underlying infrastructure, a solid understanding of networking, storage, and security is crucial to ensure that applications run smoothly and securely.

In conclusion, Kubernetes, in its essence, is more than just a tool or a platform; it's a harbinger of a new era in software design and operations. It nudges organizations towards microservices, instills application resilience, and enforces best practices in deployment and scaling. As the digital realm expands and applications become more complex, the need for a helmsman to steer the ship becomes paramount. With its rich feature set, community backing, and visionary approach, Kubernetes stands tall, guiding us through the ever-evolving seas of container orchestration. Like a trusted captain, it ensures that no matter how turbulent the waters, our applications sail smoothly, reaching the horizons of efficiency, scalability, and reliability.

Comparing Docker Swarm and Kubernetes

It is impossible to deny containerization's ascendancy in the field of software development and deployment. Coordinating and overseeing containers at scale is essential as applications expand and surroundings get more complicated. The most well-known titans in this field are Kubernetes and Docker Swarm. While both seek to simplify container orchestration, each has a unique style and approach. In order to help operations teams and developers make an informed choice, this section aims to analyze the nuances, advantages, and disadvantages of various platforms.

It's critical first to comprehend the heritage and concept of each tool. The native clustering tool for Docker, called Docker Swarm, was created with ease of use and close integration with the Docker ecosystem in mind. The company that created Docker, Docker Inc., released Swarm to give users a native orchestration tool that would blend in perfectly with the Docker environment. In contrast, Kubernetes—whose Greek name means "helmsman"—was developed at Google using ten years of experience managing large-scale production workloads. After being made available as an open-source project in 2014, Kubernetes attracted a large following and quickly became extremely popular.

Examining the features and capacities of each, it becomes clear that Kubernetes provides a more extensive range of functionalities than Docker Swarm. Kubernetes is engineered to support intricate, large-scale applications with its extensive configuration choices, self-healing capabilities, and intelligent scheduling. Docker Swarm excels in its simplicity even if it has a smaller feature set than Kubernetes. Because of Swarm's interaction with the Docker CLI, users accustomed to using Docker commands will find switching to Swarm orchestration simple.

These systems' basic building blocks have different designs and methods of operation. Kubernetes' 'pod,' which can hold one or more containers, is the smallest deployable unit. Easy networking, communication, and management of containers that require close cooperation are made possible by this encapsulation. Docker Swarm's method is easier but may be less adaptable in situations where multi-container coordination within a single deployment unit is crucial because it operates at the granularity of a single container.

The two platforms take different approaches to networking, which is a crucial component of container orchestration. By guaranteeing that each pod can connect with every other pod and hiding the underlying networking specifics, Kubernetes provides a flat networking paradigm. Although it provides great flexibility, it can also add complexity. Adhering to its minimalist philosophy, Docker Swarm offers an intuitive overlay network for services, guaranteeing communication between containers running on separate nodes.

One area in which Kubernetes excels is in its plug-and-play architecture and extensibility. Because the platform is modular in nature, customers can select and plug different components based on their needs. Kubernetes offers many options, including networking plugins, storage options, and custom schedulers. Although it is somewhat expandable, Docker Swarm's options are not as extensive as those of Kubernetes.

Another essential component of container orchestration is scalability. Although Kubernetes and Docker Swarm are both intended to scale, their approaches are different. Swarm prioritizes simple, quick scaling, with almost instantaneous container generation. Although it scales a little more slowly than Swarm, Kubernetes has more sophisticated scaling options, such as the Horizontal Pod Autoscaler, which automates scaling depending on particular parameters.

In terms of the ecosystem and community, Kubernetes is undoubtedly superior. Because of the numerous tools, extensions, and plugins that its large community has created, Kubernetes has become a center for innovation in the container orchestration space. Even with its own community and ecosystem, Docker Swarm is not nearly as dynamic and active as the Kubernetes environment.

Still, it would be a mistake to overlook the simplicity that is Docker Swarm's greatest asset. Swarm is an excellent option for groups or initiatives seeking a simple, no-frills method of container orchestration. For smaller projects or teams just getting started with orchestration, its integration with Docker tools, simple commands, and low learning curve makes it a good choice.

In conclusion, choosing between Kubernetes and Docker Swarm is not a binary option. It's a difficult decision that depends on the project's specifications, the team's experience with the tools, the need for scalability, and the preferred degree of complexity or simplicity. Kubernetes is a powerful tool appropriate for intricate, large-scale projects because of its abundant features, vast community, and versatility. Docker Swarm's simplicity, tight Docker integration, and ease of use make it the ideal choice for projects that call for a straightforward approach to orchestration.

In the field of container orchestration, these two tools are the height of innovation. The key to choose between them is being aware of one's requirements and priorities. Docker Swarm and Kubernetes are like lighthouses in the vast ocean of container orchestration, pointing development and operations teams in the right direction. The type of journey and the intended destination determine which route is taken.

CHAPTER IX

Security in Docker

Common Docker security threats

With the rise in popularity of Docker, software can now be bundled together with its dependencies into tidy, portable containers, ushering in an era of streamlined development and deployment. Significant agility and flexibility have resulted from this, particularly in cloud-native applications and microservices architectures. But like any technology, Docker has some security drawbacks in addition to its advantages. Any developer or business looking to leverage containers' capability without unintentionally creating vulnerabilities must know these concerns.

The shared kernel architecture of Docker is the main source of security issues. Containers share the host's operating system kernel, in contrast to typical virtual machines, which separate the guest's operating system from the host. This implies that a malicious entity may be able to access the host or other containers that are running on it if it can escape from a container. A single virtual machine's blast radius is substantially smaller than the blast radius of a container compromise.

The escalation of privileges within containers poses an analogous issue. Docker containers used to operate with elevated rights by default, which might have given malicious programs greater access than necessary. Despite the recent trend towards more restricted Docker configurations, many installations can still be running containers with higher access than necessary. For example, running a container as root could make it easier for a malicious program to have a big impact if it finds a way to take advantage of a weakness in the container.

Since images are the fundamental building pieces of containers, their security must be prioritized. Using old or unreliable images in the Docker ecosystem is a prevalent security risk. It is common for developers to download images from public repositories like Docker Hub without doing any content filtering or integrity checks. The images might include malicious malware, known vulnerabilities, or out-of-date software. Organizations run the danger of deploying vulnerable containers from the start if appropriate governance and checks aren't in place.

Runtime threats are still a problem, even with safe, current images. The way containers behave while they're operating could reveal security holes. For example, sensitive data leakage can occur from containers not sufficiently isolated from the host system or one another. Analogously, unsecure setups, including unencrypted inter-container communication, can provide doors for man-in-the-middle attacks and data interception.

Additionally, the API for Docker, which serves as a conduit for container orchestration and communication, may be targeted. Attackers seeking to modify or obtain insights into the operating containers may find the API to be an attractive target if appropriate access controls and authentication procedures are not in place. By overloading the Docker daemon, a hacked API may result in data breaches, illegal container launches, or even denial-of-service attacks.

The networking features of Docker give rise to another potential source of attack. Several networking modes, including bridge, host, and overlay, are offered by Docker; each has unique security consequences. In host mode, for example, containers share the networking namespace with the host, which could make them more vulnerable to attacks. Networking misconfigurations can result in unintentional service disclosure, container-to-container listening, or even unapproved access to the host's network.

Additionally, as Docker has become more popular, platforms and technologies for orchestration such as Docker Swarm, Kubernetes, and OpenShift have proliferated. Although these tools help container deployments become more automated and scalable, they also add another level of complexity to the security landscape. Large-scale breaches can result from misconfigurations of these platforms, such as leaving management interfaces open without the necessary authentication.

Many applications require persistent storage; however, it is not without its difficulties. Data integrity and confidentiality must be carefully managed when using Docker volumes, which are used to store data after the container lifespan. Inadequate volume management may result in unapproved data alteration or leakage. Furthermore, sensitive data within volumes becomes readily accessible for attackers if it isn't encrypted while it's in transit and at rest.

Adding to these difficulties is the possibility that conventional intrusion detection and security monitoring systems are ill-suited to handle the specifics of containerized settings. Anomaly detection can be challenging due to the transient nature of containers, their density, and their quick scale-up/scale-down cycles.

In conclusion, there are security risks associated with Docker and containerization as a whole, even though they can potentially transform how we develop and distribute software completely. The threats span from runtime issues and misconfigurations to fundamental elements like image security. A multifaceted strategy is needed to ensure Docker security, including image screening, least privilege principles implementation, networking and Docker API security, and the use of specific security tools designed for container settings. As with any technology, the best protection against security threats are vigilance, continual education, and adoption of best practices. Accepting Docker's benefits does not imply disregarding its drawbacks; instead, it means navigating around it while being well aware of any approaching hazards.

Best practices for secure containerization

In the contemporary world of software development, containerization, spearheaded by technologies like Docker, has become a cornerstone. Containers offer an elegant solution to software deployment's most pressing challenges: ensuring consistency across multiple environments, achieving faster boot times, and optimizing resource usage. However, as with any technological advancement, this comes with security implications. The containers' transient nature, shared kernel model, and intricate orchestration mechanisms can be both a boon and a bane. The beauty of containerization can quickly turn sour if security is an afterthought. This section highlights the best practices that should be ingrained in every developer and administrator's workflow to ensure secure container deployments.

The first and perhaps most crucial principle is the concept of "least privilege." Every container should be granted only those absolutely essential permissions for its function. This often translates to running containers as non-root users in the Docker ecosystem. Containers initiated with root privileges can pose significant threats if compromised, as they could potentially gain access to the host system. By using a non-root user, the potential damage an attacker can inflict is substantially limited.

Next on the agenda is image provenance. Containers spring to life from images, making image security paramount. Relying on images from unknown or untrusted sources can be a recipe for disaster. It's essential to either use official images or, better yet, build custom images from trusted base images. Additionally, regularly scanning these images for vulnerabilities ensures that potential security flaws are identified and rectified promptly. Tools like Clair or Trivy can assist in this vulnerability scanning process, offering insights into possible weak points in the image.

While on the subject of images, it's worth noting the importance of minimalism. Every additional package or library that's packed into an image is a potential vulnerability waiting to be exploited. Adopting a minimalist approach by including only essential components makes containers lightweight and reduces their attack surface. Base images like Alpine Linux, known for their minimal footprint, can be a good starting point.

Another fundamental aspect of container security is isolation. Docker, by design, offers a decent level of isolation between containers using namespaces. However, tools like gVisor or Kata Containers can be employed for applications requiring an extra layer of security. These tools provide an additional isolation layer, ensuring that the attacker remains confined even if a container is breached and cannot tamper with the host or other containers.

The Docker daemon, the heart that powers Docker's operations, should be shielded with care. Binding to a Unix socket, as opposed to a TCP port, is a more secure default binding method for the Docker daemon. If, for some reason, binding to a TCP port becomes necessary, ensure it's protected using TLS and is not exposed beyond trusted networks. Furthermore, the Docker API, which the daemon exposes, should be protected with rigorous access controls, allowing only trusted entities to interact with it.

Networking, an intricate component of Docker's ecosystem, demands careful attention. By default, Docker employs a bridge network, which provides a private internal IP to each container. While this mode is generally safe for most applications, Docker's host networking mode should be avoided for containers that demand heightened security. In situations where inter-container communication is necessary, encrypted channels, potentially facilitated by tools like Calico or Cilium, should be the norm.

Persistent storage, while crucial for maintaining data across container lifecycles, poses its challenges. When employing Docker volumes, it's essential to make sure that sensitive data is encrypted at rest and in transit. Tools like HashiCorp's Vault can assist in managing and encrypting secrets, ensuring they don't fall into the wrong hands.

Lastly, monitoring and logging cannot be overstated. Containers, by their very nature, are dynamic entities that can be initiated or terminated in the blink of an eye. Traditional security monitoring tools may not be fully attuned to this rapid lifecycle. Embracing tools designed for container environments, like Falco or Sysdig, can offer insights into suspicious activities within the container ecosystem. Comprehensive logging, coupled with alert mechanisms, ensures that anomalies are detected and brought to immediate attention.

In conclusion, the realm of containerization, while brimming with potential, has its pitfalls. Security in this space is not just a checkbox but a continuous endeavor. From the images that give birth to containers, through their lifecycle, to their eventual termination, security should be a guiding beacon. By embracing best practices like least privilege, image provenance, minimalism, isolation, secure networking, and vigilant monitoring, organizations and developers can confidently navigate the containerized landscape. In a world where agility is often at odds with security, containerization done right offers a harmonious path, marrying the best of both worlds.

Tools for scanning and monitoring Docker deployments

The containerization wave, championed by Docker, has brought unprecedented efficiency and consistency in software deployment. But, as is often the case with emerging technologies, the rapid adoption of containers has also opened up a new set of challenges, particularly regarding security and monitoring. Just as a ship's captain needs tools to navigate treacherous waters, developers and administrators require specialized tools to ensure their Docker deployments are secure, efficient, and operational. This section dives deep into some prominent tools that have emerged as frontrunners in Docker scanning and monitoring, exploring their capabilities, use cases, and overall impact on the container ecosystem.

Starting with security, the first line of defense regarding Docker deployments is ensuring that the container images are free from vulnerabilities. Enter Clair. Developed by CoreOS, Clair is an open-source project designed to scan container images for known security vulnerabilities. With an ever-growing database of vulnerabilities sourced from multiple databases, Clair comprehensively assesses potential threats in an image. Another equally notable tool in this space is Trivy. Hailing from the stables of Aqua Security, Trivy boasts an easy-to-use, comprehensive vulnerability scanner specifically designed for containers. Its ability to integrate seamlessly with continuous integration (CI) pipelines makes it a favorite among developers aiming for a "shift-left" security paradigm.

Beyond image scanning, runtime security holds paramount importance. Falco, a Cloud-Native Computing Foundation incubating project, rises to this challenge. Falco monitors container runtime behaviors and raises alerts for any suspicious or anomalous activities. With a rich set of rules and the flexibility to craft custom policies, Falco ensures that breaches are detected and mitigated in real-time.

However, security is just one facet of the puzzle. Effective monitoring and observability are crucial to ensure that Docker deployments operate at their peak performance. Prometheus, an open-source monitoring and also alerting toolkit, has quickly become the gold standard in the container monitoring space. Its multidimensional data model, flexible query language, and integration capabilities make it an indispensable tool for gauging container health and performance. When paired with Grafana, a platform for analytics and monitoring, users get a powerful combination that offers rich visualizations and in-depth insights into their Docker deployments.

cAdvisor (short for Container Advisor) is another invaluable tool developed by Google. Integrated into the Kubelet in a Kubernetes setup, cAdvisor provides users with details about resource usage and performance characteristics of their running containers. It stands out for its ability to gather complete container information without any additional configuration.

As Docker deployments scale, so does the need for comprehensive logging. ELK Stack, which stands for Elasticsearch, Logstash, and Kibana, offers a compelling solution. While Elasticsearch is a search and analytics engine, Logstash is responsible for server-side data processing, and Kibana provides the visualization layer. Together, they offer a centralized logging solution, ensuring administrators and developers can quickly trace issues or glean insights from their Docker logs.

For teams that prioritize an all-in-one solution, Sysdig shines through. Offering security scanning and runtime monitoring, Sysdig presents a unified platform to meet the diverse needs of Docker deployments. With deep visibility into container performance, security policies to guard against threats, and an intuitive user interface, Sysdig has established itself as a comprehensive tool for teams serious about their container health.

Discussion on Docker monitoring would only be complete with mentioning Docker's in-built monitoring tools. Commands like docker stats or docker top offer immediate insights into a container's CPU, memory, and network usage. While they may not boast the extensive features of dedicated monitoring solutions, these native tools are handy for quick checks or troubleshooting.

In conclusion, as Docker continues to dominate the containerization space, the ecosystem of tools surrounding it has flourished. These tools, each with its strengths, collectively ensure that Docker deployments remain secure, efficient, and operational. Whether it's the security diligence offered by Clair and Trivy, the runtime observability provided by Prometheus and cAdvisor, or the holistic approach of Sysdig, the tooling landscape for Docker is both diverse and robust.

For organizations and developers navigating the Docker waters, these tools aren't just luxuries but necessities. They act as the compass, the radar, and the lifeboats ensuring that the ship not only stays its course but also tackles any storm that comes its way. As the famous adage goes, "A craftsman is only as good as his tools." In Docker deployments, having the proper scanning and monitoring tools isn't just about optimizing operations; it's about securing the foundation of modern software.

CHAPTER X

Advanced Docker Techniques

Docker in microservices architecture

Within the quickly changing field of software development, two significant shifts have dominated recent discussions and practices: the rise of microservices architecture and the emergence of Docker as a powerful containerization tool. Intricately linked in their mutual objectives and benefits, Docker and microservices have forged a new frontier in creating scalable, resilient, and maintainable software solutions. This section explores the synergy between Docker and microservices, elucidating how they complement each other and examining their combined impact on contemporary software delivery paradigms.

Microservices architecture is rooted in decomposing a traditionally monolithic application into a suite of smaller, loosely coupled services. Each service caters to a specific business capability and operates independently, communicating with its counterparts via lightweight mechanisms like HTTP-based APIs. Such decomposition offers several advantages: it provides teams the freedom to choose the best technology stack for each service, facilitates better fault isolation, and enables granular scaling based on the varying workloads of different services.

However, with the plethora of benefits microservices promise, they also introduce a unique set of challenges. Differing technology stacks and configurations, the need for isolated environments for each service, and the complexities of service deployment and scaling are just some of the hurdles that teams face. Here, Docker's capabilities shine through, providing a lifeline for effective microservices development and deployment.

Docker, at its core, is a containerization platform. Containers enable developers to package an application and its dependencies, libraries, and configurations into a single unit, ensuring consistency across various environments. This uniformity is invaluable in a microservices world where services developed by different teams and using diverse technology stacks must coexist harmoniously. By using Docker containers, teams can be assured that their microservice will run consistently, regardless of where the container is deployed, be it a developer's local machine, test environment, or production server.

Furthermore, Docker's lightweight nature offers an immediate solution to one of the microservices' main challenges: resource overhead. Unlike traditional virtualization, which requires running multiple instances of an operating system, Docker containers share the same OS kernel and isolate the application processes from each other. This ensures that microservices, when containerized using

Docker, are lightweight and quick to start, scale, and stop, mirroring the agility that microservices aim to achieve.

In addition to providing a consistent and lightweight runtime environment, Docker offers tools and practices that simplify the orchestration of microservices. Docker Compose enable developers to define and run multi-container applications, ensuring that microservices and their dependencies are coordinated. For more extensive deployments, orchestration tools like Docker Swarm or Kubernetes can manage, scale, and maintain containerized microservices, handling tasks like load balancing, service discovery, and auto-scaling. Tightly integrated with Docker, these orchestration tools ensure that as microservices grow in number and complexity, they remain manageable and resilient.

The transient nature of containers dovetails perfectly with the dynamic lifecycle of microservices. As microservices must be frequently updated, scaled, or even retired, Docker containers can be effortlessly spun up or torn down, ensuring that the ecosystem remains agile and responsive to business needs. This elasticity, combined with Docker's versioning capabilities, means that rolling updates, rollbacks, and blue-green deployments become straightforward, reducing the risk associated with frequent releases.

From a developer's perspective, Docker also amplifies the microservices mantra of autonomy and decentralization. By containerizing their microservice, developers can work in an environment that precisely mirrors production, eliminating the age-old "it works on my machine" problem. This parity boosts developer productivity and fosters a culture of responsibility, where developers can own their microservices from development to production.

In the grand tapestry of modern software development, Docker and microservices represent threads of innovation and pragmatism. Woven together, they create a fabric that is robust yet flexible, structured yet adaptable. While microservices provide the architectural paradigm shift, focusing on modularization, decentralization, and scalability, Docker offers the tools and practices that bring this vision to life, ensuring that microservices are not just a theoretical construct but a tangible, operational reality.

In conclusion, the relationship between Docker and microservices symbolizes the broader trends in software development: a move towards granularity, agility, and autonomy. As organizations seek ways to deliver value faster, more reliably, and at scale, the confluence of Docker and microservices offers a proven path. It's a symbiosis that defines the current state of software development and promises to shape its future, guiding developers and businesses toward new horizons of innovation, efficiency, and growth.

Multi-stage builds for optimized images

Ever since its inception, Docker has radically transformed the software development landscape. By packaging applications along with their dependencies into containers, Docker guarantees consistency across various deployment environments. However, as with every technological tool, there's always room for optimization, and when it comes to Docker, image size stands out as a critical parameter. Large images consume more storage and can slow down the deployment process, especially in environments where bandwidth is a concern. This challenge brings forth the significance of multi-stage builds, a feature in Docker that allows developers to create leaner, more optimized images. This section delves deep into the concept of multi-stage builds, exploring how they work, the benefits they confer, and their transformative impact on the containerization process.

At its core, multi-stage builds address a fundamental discrepancy between the build and runtime environments. Often, building an application requires numerous dependencies, tools, and intermediate files. These might include compilers, libraries, source code, or even test tools. However, once the build process is complete and we have the final executable or application, many of these build-time dependencies are no longer needed for running the application. Traditional single-stage Docker builds do not distinguish between these two environments, often leading to bloated images packed with unnecessary files.

Enter multi-stage builds. This Docker feature allows developers to use multiple FROM statements within a single Dockerfile. Each FROM instruction can be considered a distinct stage of the build process. Developers can use different base images, install various tools, and execute unique commands in each stage. However, only the artifacts or files explicitly copied from one stage to another persist, while everything else is discarded. This provides a structured way to separate the build environment from the runtime environment, ensuring that the final image contains only what's absolutely essential for the application's execution.

For instance, consider a C++ application. The build process might require the entire GCC toolchain, libraries, headers, and the application's source code. However, the runtime might only need the compiled binary. Using multi-stage builds, the Dockerfile can have a stage that uses an image with GCC to compile the application, and then, another stage starts with a minimal base image where the compiled binary is copied. The resulting Docker image would only contain the binary and necessary runtime dependencies, excluding the hefty GCC toolchain and source files.

The benefits of multi-stage builds are manifold. Firstly, and most evidently, they lead to significantly smaller image sizes. Reduced image sizes translate to faster pull and push times, making deployments, scaling, and rollbacks more efficient. This is especially valuable in cloud-native environments where services might be frequently deployed, scaled, or moved across nodes.

Moreover, smaller images have a cascading security advantage. The potential attack surface is reduced with fewer components and software packed in the image. Also, by excluding unnecessary tools and dependencies, you inherently exclude potential vulnerabilities associated with them. In cybersecurity, where every layer of defense counts, multi-stage builds act as a proactive step towards hardening the application environment.

From a resource consumption standpoint, smaller images mean quicker container start-up times. Especially for use cases like serverless computing, where container start-up latency plays a pivotal role in the user experience, multi-stage builds can differentiate between an application being deemed performant or sluggish.

However, while the benefits are compelling, there are considerations to consider. The multi-stage build process requires meticulous planning. Developers must judiciously decide which artifacts or files must be carried over between stages, ensuring the final image is both lightweight and functional. There's also a learning curve involved, especially for developers new to Docker, as they grapple with the intricacies of drafting an optimized Dockerfile that harnesses the full power of multi-stage builds.

In conclusion, multi-stage builds in Docker represent a paradigm shift in how we think about containerization. They challenge the erstwhile monolithic approach, advocating for a more granular, optimized, and deliberate method of building images. In an era where efficiency, speed, and security are paramount, multi-stage builds emerge as a cornerstone technique for modern software delivery. They epitomize the ethos of doing more with less, ensuring that Docker containers, known for their portability and consistency, are optimized for size and performance. As containerization continues to be the backbone of contemporary application deployment strategies, multi-stage builds, emphasizing optimization, are poised to play an increasingly central role in shaping the future of software development and delivery.

Tips and tricks for power users

When Solomon Hykes introduced Docker in 2013, the software development world encountered a transformation. Docker's promise of "Build, Ship, and Run Any App, Anywhere" was more than just a slogan—it was a vision of streamlined development, testing, and deployment. As Docker gained traction, the early adopters, those power users, began exploring beyond the basics. They delved into Docker's intricacies, finding ways to extract more efficiency, flexibility, and power. This section seeks to impart some of that distilled wisdom, shedding light on the lesser-known corners of Docker that power users have come to cherish.

One of the foundational elements of Docker's power is its command-line interface (CLI). While graphical user interfaces (GUIs) like Docker Desktop offer convenience, the CLI is where power users often find their stride. With many commands and options at their fingertips, knowing a few handy CLI tricks can significantly enhance productivity. For instance, docker system df gives a quick overview of disk usage, helping users identify and remove unneeded images or containers, while docker ps -q yields just the container IDs, which are useful for batch operations.

A key area where Docker shines is its ability to create isolated environments, but sometimes, one might want to go beyond the default isolation. This is where the --network flag comes into play. Power users leverage custom bridge networks to create isolated environments for containers, ensuring that applications in development don't inadvertently interact with others. Additionally, using Docker's host networking mode (--network host) can sometimes improve network performance, especially in cases where minimal network latency is crucial.

Image management is another realm where Docker offers vast possibilities. Power users frequently employ the docker image prune and docker container prune commands to clean up unused images and containers. However, the real magic lies in using specific image hashes (obtained using docker images --no-trunc) to roll back to earlier versions of an application. This method offers an efficient mechanism to manage versions without relying heavily on tags.

Speaking of efficiency, Docker's build cache is a boon. When Docker builds an image, it caches each layer. If a particular layer hasn't changed in subsequent builds, Docker reuses it from the cache, speeding up the build process. Power users often strategically order their Dockerfile instructions, placing the most frequently changed instructions towards the end. This approach maximizes cache utilization, leading to faster build times.

On the topic of Dockerfiles, one cannot emphasize enough the utility of .dockerignore. Just as .gitignore prevents unnecessary files from being versioned, .dockerignore ensures unwanted files don't end up in the Docker image. Power users curate their .dockerignore files meticulously, ensuring only essential files are included in the build context. This reduces image size and accelerates the build process by avoiding the transfer of unnecessary files.

Container introspection is an area often overlooked but holds immense power. Commands like docker top CONTAINER_ID provide insight into the processes running inside a container, while docker stats offer a real-time stream of container resource usage statistics. Power users turn to tools like ctop or docker-slim for deeper insights, which provide advanced monitoring and optimization capabilities.

Power users also know that while Docker excels at isolation, there are times when direct interaction with a container becomes necessary. The docker exec command is a favorite here, allowing users to execute commands inside a running container. This capability is invaluable for debugging or when a closer inspection of the container's environment is warranted.

Docker Compose, often the unsung hero, gets its due attention from power users. Beyond the basics of defining multi-container applications, advanced features like depends_on, combined with health checks, allow for sophisticated orchestration ensuring services start in the desired order and only when dependencies are healthy and ready.

In conclusion, while Docker's surface-level advantages like portability and consistency are well-recognized, the true power lies in its depths. The aforementioned tips and tricks are just the tip of the iceberg. As with any tool, the more one uses Docker, the more nuances and capabilities one discovers. The software's versatility and depth are testaments to its transformative potential. With their relentless pursuit of optimization, power users continue to push Docker's boundaries, ensuring that this containerization giant remains at the forefront of software development innovation. Their explorations and insights contribute to Docker's evolving ecosystem and serve as a beacon, guiding others toward mastering this powerful tool.

CHAPTER XI

Real-World Case Studies

Successful implementations of Docker in the industry

In software development and deployment, few innovations have made as significant an impact in recent years as Docker. Its rise to prominence isn't merely a result of its revolutionary technology but also its successful applications across various industries. This section delves into some of Docker's most notable industry implementations, showcasing its transformative potential and the multiple avenues where it has been employed to great effect.

The story of Docker's industry success begins in the tech giants' domains. Netflix, a behemoth in the streaming service sector, has been at the forefront of cloud and microservices adoption. Docker has been pivotal in Netflix's transition towards a scalable, resilient, and highly available infrastructure. By containerizing their applications, Netflix achieved consistent environments from development through production, mitigating the "it works on my machine" dilemma that plagues many development teams. Docker containers and orchestration tools allowed Netflix to manage its vast microservices architecture, ensuring smooth streaming experiences for millions of global users.

PayPal offers another testament to Docker's industry prowess. With a complex infrastructure handling billions of transactions, the financial giant needed a solution to streamline development and reduce deployment inconsistencies. Docker emerged as the hero. Introducing Docker containers enabled PayPal to encapsulate their applications and dependencies cohesively. As a result, developers could work in isolated environments without interference, test their applications consistently, and deploy faster, meeting the high demands of the ever-evolving fintech sector.

The gaming industry, known for its rapid iterations and need for high-performance, also saw Docker's benefits. The makers of the immensely popular "League of Legends," Riot Games, used Docker to expedite their deployment and continuous integration procedures. The complexities of game development, with its vast array of assets, libraries, and services, found a solution in Docker's containerized approach. This sped up their build and deployment times and reduced inconsistencies, ensuring that gamers worldwide experienced fewer glitches and more seamless gameplay.

Outside of entertainment and finance, Docker's merits shine brightly in academia and research. Cornell University, a renowned institution in the research sphere, leveraged Docker in its pursuit of advanced computational studies. Their "Whole Tale" project aimed to make research more transparent and reproducible. Docker containers became the backbone of this initiative, encapsulating computational environments, data, and tools into shareable units. This ensured that research outputs were shared as raw data or results and as fully replicable computational tales.

In the realm of e-commerce, Docker's success stories are aplenty. One example is Shopify, a platform that powers numerous online stores worldwide. A more flexible, scalable, and consistent development environment became paramount as their user base grew. Enter Docker. Shopify's transition to a containerized infrastructure, orchestrated by Kubernetes, allowed them to manage thousands of shops with diverse needs. The agility brought forth by Docker ensured that new features, fixes, and updates could roll out rapidly and reliably, keeping online businesses running smoothly.

With its critical services and stringent compliance requirements, the healthcare sector might seem an unlikely candidate for Docker's innovations, but the reality is quite the contrary. Cerner, a global leader in health technology, adopted Docker to address the challenges of developing healthcare applications that are both robust and compliant. By containerizing their applications, Cerner could ensure that the environment remained consistent throughout the software lifecycle. This reduced the chances of deployment errors and simplified compliance, as regulators could be assured of the software's behavior across different stages.

One of Docker's more unconventional yet impactful implementations is in the aerospace industry. NASA's Jet Propulsion Laboratory (JPL) turned to Docker for mission analysis and trajectory design. The intricate simulations and computations required for space missions found an ally in Docker's container technology. By creating consistent, reproducible environments, Docker ensured that the simulations run by JPL were accurate and reliable, a necessity when planning missions to the far reaches of our solar system.

In conclusion, Docker's industry implementations paint a picture of versatility, resilience, and innovation. Docker's influence is ubiquitous, from streaming services to financial transactions, game development to groundbreaking research, online shopping to life-saving healthcare, and even the vast expanse of space. Its consistency, portability, and scalability promise has been realized across diverse sectors, highlighting its transformative power. As industries evolve and new challenges emerge, Docker's successful implementations are a testament to its potential, beckoning more organizations to embrace its revolution.

Addressing challenges with Docker

Docker, with its promise of containerization and the streamlining of software deployments, has become a cornerstone in the modern software development lifecycle. Its adoption has accelerated application development and deployment, enabling consistency and reproducibility across diverse computing environments. Yet, as with any technological innovation, Docker has challenges. This section seeks to explore some of the more pressing issues that users may encounter when working with Docker, and to provide insight into how these challenges can be addressed to utilize the full potential of containerized solutions.

One of the primary challenges faced in the Docker ecosystem revolves around image size. By nature, Docker images aim to encapsulate an application and all its dependencies. However, as developers add tools, libraries, and other resources, the image size can balloon, leading to slower deployment times and increased storage costs. Addressing this challenge requires a meticulous approach to image creation. Developers should be wary of including unnecessary components and should leverage multi-stage builds. This approach involves using intermediary images to compile or prepare data and copying only the essentials into a final, smaller image. Such practices ensure that the end image is lightweight, without extraneous baggage.

Another significant challenge is the complexity of orchestration. As applications grow and the number of containers multiplies, managing inter-container communication, scaling, and resilience becomes intricate. While Docker provides native tools like Docker Compose and Docker Swarm for orchestration, many users opt for more advanced platforms like Kubernetes. Choosing the right orchestration platform depends on the scale and complexity of the deployment. Nevertheless, investing time in understanding the nuances of these tools, defining clear service boundaries, and ensuring robust monitoring can alleviate many orchestration-related challenges.

Security is paramount in any software endeavor, and Docker is no exception. The dynamic nature of containers, often spun up and terminated in response to load, can make traditional security monitoring and intrusion detection methods less effective. Ensuring container security involves multiple layers of defense. Starting from the base, using minimal and verified base images can reduce the potential attack surface. Regularly scanning images for vulnerabilities, employing read-only filesystems for containers, and following the principle of least privilege for container processes are just a few strategies to bolster security. Additionally, specialized tools like Aqua Trivy or Anchore can be harnessed to scan containers for known vulnerabilities, further fortifying the environment.

Docker's ephemeral nature can sometimes be a double-edged sword, especially when considering data persistence. Containers, by design, are transient. Any data generated or modified within a container can be lost if that container is terminated. Addressing this challenge requires a keen understanding of Docker volumes and bind mounts. By effectively using these, developers can ensure that critical data persists beyond the lifecycle of individual containers. Depending on the nature of the data and the application, developers might also need to look into distributed storage solutions that are resilient, scalable, and compatible with the container ecosystem.

Interrelated with the challenge of data persistence is the topic of networking. Containers within a Docker environment often need to communicate with each other and with external entities. Ensuring efficient and secure container networking involves understanding Docker's built-in network drivers, defining clear network policies, and possibly leveraging third-party solutions for advanced requirements. Challenges like inter-container latency, network isolation, and service discovery can be addressed through careful network planning and the use of tools like Calico or Flannel.

Lastly, one cannot overlook the learning curve associated with Docker. For teams and individuals accustomed to traditional virtualization or monolithic architectures, transitioning to Docker's microservices and container-driven paradigm can be daunting.

Addressing this challenge is, in many ways, a matter of time and education. Comprehensive documentation, hands-on workshops, and real-world project experience can help bridge the knowledge gap. The Docker community, being vibrant and collaborative, offers a plethora of resources, from online forums to tutorials, aiding those on their containerization journey.

In conclusion, Docker's transformative potential in software development and deployment is undeniable. It offers a path to consistency, scalability, and efficiency. However, the journey is not without its hurdles. By recognizing and addressing challenges related to image size, orchestration complexity, security, data persistence, networking, and the inherent learning curve, teams can confidently navigate the seas of innovation. In doing so, they can leverage Docker to its fullest, ensuring that their software solutions are robust, agile, and poised to meet the ever-evolving demands of the digital age.

Lessons learned from real-world deployments

Docker's emergence as a frontrunner in containerization is unquestionable in the kaleidoscope of software development tools and methodologies. Its promise of simplified deployments, scalability, and environment consistency has beckoned enterprises and individual developers alike. Yet, as with any tool, real-world implementation reveals a spectrum of successes, surprises, and setbacks. This section captures the most valuable lessons learned from diverse Docker deployments in the industry.

The initial allure of Docker lies in its promise of environmental consistency. Developers have long grappled with the dreaded "it works on my machine" syndrome. Docker's premise to encapsulate applications and their dependencies in an isolated environment, ensuring consistency across development, testing, and production, is undeniably attractive. However, real-world deployments emphasize the importance of regularly updating and maintaining Docker images. Stale images, laden with outdated libraries and software patches, can introduce vulnerabilities. Enterprises have learned that regular audits, vulnerability scanning, and disciplined updates are paramount to keeping Docker deployments secure and consistent.

Regarding scalability, Docker offers significant advantages, particularly when combined with orchestration tools. Yet, real-world deployments have underscored the importance of meticulous resource management. Containers, while lightweight compared to traditional virtual machines, can still become resource-intensive when not configured appropriately. One particularly poignant lesson from industry deployments is the caution against over-allocating resources to individual containers, be it CPU, memory, or storage. Such over-allocation can lead to suboptimal utilization and, in extreme cases, system bottlenecks.

A recurring theme from Docker deployments is the nuanced challenge of data persistence. The transient nature of containers means that without deliberate planning, data can be lost when a container is terminated. Many enterprises have learned the importance of effectively leveraging Docker volumes to ensure data continuity. Additionally, there's a growing realization that while

Docker provides robust solutions for application deployment, it may not always be the best solution for data-intensive applications or databases. Hence, striking a balance between containerized applications and traditional database management systems often emerges as a pragmatic approach.

Networking, a cornerstone of any software deployment, poses its own set of challenges in the Docker universe. Lessons from the field highlight the intricacies of managing inter-container communication, especially in deployments where containers span multiple hosts or even cloud providers. While powerful, the built-in Docker networking modes may not always suffice for complex deployments. As such, real-world Docker implementations often rely on third-party plugins or tools to ensure seamless and secure networking. This dependence underscores the importance of having a versatile toolset and being adaptable to evolving project requirements.

Another valuable insight from Docker deployments pertains to the integration of legacy systems. Docker's modus operandi aligns seamlessly with microservices and cloud-native applications. However, integrating Docker with older, monolithic systems can be laborious. Here, lessons from the industry emphasize a phased approach. Instead of an aggressive overhaul, organizations have found value in incrementally containerizing components of legacy systems, thereby reducing risk and ensuring uninterrupted service continuity.

Monitoring and logging are indispensable facets of any software deployment. With Docker, the dynamic nature of containers—

constantly being created and destroyed—introduces unique monitoring challenges. Traditional tools and approaches may not suffice. Organizations have learned the significance of investing in container-specific monitoring solutions through third-party tools or custom solutions. Logging, especially centralized logging, emerges as a recurring theme, enabling developers to trace issues across a fleet of ephemeral containers.

The human aspect of Docker deployments cannot be overstated. The technical complexities, while surmountable, pale in comparison to the challenges of upskilling, training, and fostering a culture receptive to Docker's methodologies. Enterprises have realized that Docker's successful implementation extends beyond technical prowess; it demands an organizational mindset shift. Regular training sessions, workshops, and community engagements have proven invaluable in easing this transition.

In conclusion, Docker, with its transformative potential, is reshaping the software development landscape. However, as organizations navigate their Docker journey, they face myriad challenges, each offering invaluable lessons. Whether it's the nuances of resource management, the intricacies of networking, the challenges of data persistence, or the overarching demand for a cultural shift, these lessons shape future deployments. By heeding these insights, organizations can harness Docker's full potential, ensuring that their software solutions are innovative, robust, scalable, and tailored to the ever-evolving demands of the digital realm.

CHAPTER XII

The Future of
Docker and Containerization

Emerging trends in the container ecosystem

In the dynamic world of software development, containerization has evolved into a transformative force, reshaping how applications are developed, deployed, and scaled. At the epicenter of this revolution stands Docker, a tool that pioneered containerization for the masses. Yet, as with any vibrant technological domain, the container ecosystem constantly evolves, spurred by many emerging trends. These trends, driven by industry demands, technological advancements, and community innovations, offer a glimpse into the future trajectory of containerization and its ever-expanding influence on the broader IT landscape.

The first significant trend is the proliferation of container orchestration platforms. While Docker introduced the world to the concept of containers, managing these containers at scale necessitates specialized tools. Docker Swarm emerged as Docker's native solution, but Kubernetes has primarily dominated the container orchestration domain. Initially developed by Google,

Kubernetes offers a robust platform to manage, scale, and monitor containerized applications. Yet, the orchestration arena is far from static. Projects like Nomad from HashiCorp are steadily gaining traction, introducing innovations and features that challenge the prevailing norms. This growing diversity in orchestration tools highlights the industry's appetite for specialized, scalable, and flexible solutions that cater to a variety of deployment scenarios.

Another discernible trend is the focus on container security. As containers become mainstream, they inevitably become targets for malicious actors. The container ecosystem was initially criticized for potential security lapses, particularly around container isolation and image vulnerabilities. Recognizing this, the community and industry have galvanized efforts toward bolstering container security. Tools like Aqua Security, Twistlock, and Clair have emerged, offering specialized solutions to scan, monitor, and safeguard containerized deployments. Moreover, a more disciplined approach to using and updating container images, combined with best practices like minimalistic base images and regular vulnerability scanning, is becoming the industry norm.

The realm of serverless computing is also interweaving with the container ecosystem. Serverless architectures, where developers focus solely on code, leaving infrastructure management to cloud providers, resonate with the container philosophy of abstraction and simplicity. As a result, platforms like AWS Lambda, Azure Functions, and Google Cloud Functions increasingly offer container support, allowing developers to deploy containerized applications in a serverless environment. This confluence of serverless and containers epitomizes the broader industry trend of abstracting infrastructure complexities, enabling developers to focus on delivering value through code.

Edge computing is another domain where the container ecosystem is making inroads. As the demand for localized computing intensifies, especially in IoT deployments, containers emerge as a natural solution. Their lightweight nature and ability to package all dependencies make them ideal for edge devices with limited resources. Projects like K3s, a lightweight Kubernetes distribution, are explicitly designed for edge and resource-constrained environments, further underscoring containers' growing influence in this domain.

The concept of GitOps is also infusing the container ecosystem. GitOps, an approach where Git repositories serve as the single source of truth for infrastructure and deployment, aligns perfectly with containerized CI/CD pipelines. Tools like ArgoCD and Flux have emerged, championing the GitOps cause in the container domain. By leveraging GitOps, organizations can achieve unparalleled transparency, consistency, and auditability in their containerized deployments.

Service mesh technology is another noteworthy trend. As microservices architectures, often deployed using containers, become ubiquitous, inter-service communication, monitoring, and security challenges become pronounced. With tools like Istio and Linkerd, service meshes offer solutions to these challenges, providing a dedicated infrastructure layer to handle service-to-service communication. In essence, service meshes elevate the container ecosystem, addressing inherent challenges and setting the stage for more complex, scalable, and resilient deployments.

Lastly, IT infrastructures' sustainability and environmental impact have garnered attention, and the container ecosystem is no exception. By virtue of their efficient resource utilization, containers are being recognized for their potential to reduce carbon footprints. By minimizing the need for sprawling infrastructures and optimizing hardware utilization, containerized deployments can contribute to greener, more sustainable IT practices.

In conclusion, while rooted in the foundational principles introduced by Docker, the container ecosystem is in a state of flux, shaped by emerging trends and innovations. The landscape is diverse and dynamic from the evolution of orchestration tools and the increasing focus on security to the confluence with serverless, edge computing, GitOps, service meshes, and sustainability. These trends highlight the container ecosystem's adaptability and its growing influence on shaping the future of IT and software development. As containers continue to permeate every facet of IT, understanding and embracing these trends becomes essential for organizations and developers aiming to stay ahead of the curve in this exhilarating journey of continuous innovation.

How Docker fits into the larger cloud-native landscape

The modern era of software development, characterized by scalable, resilient, and agile systems, is deeply intertwined with the cloud-native paradigm. Embracing microservices, continuous deployment, orchestration, and other such practices, the cloud-native approach seeks to optimize systems for cloud environments, benefiting from the scalability, resilience, and agility inherent to cloud platforms. Central to this transformative movement stands Docker, a tool that has become synonymous with containerization. Yet, Docker's role in this vast landscape extends beyond merely encapsulating container applications. Its influence permeates cloud-native development's architectural, operational, and cultural facets, rendering it a pivotal element in this expansive ecosystem.

To appreciate Docker's position in the cloud-native milieu, one must first understand the foundational principles of cloud-native architectures. Cloud-native systems prioritize modularity, scalability, and resilience. They are designed to run seamlessly in cloud environments, leveraging the inherent benefits of these platforms. Microservices architectures, where applications are decomposed into loosely coupled, independently deployable services, are a staple of the cloud-native approach. This architecture facilitates scalability, as each service can scale independently, and resilience, as failures in one service don't necessarily compromise the entire system.

Enter Docker, and its pivotal role becomes apparent. Docker offers an ideal medium to package, deploy, and run these microservices. By encapsulating each service in a container, Docker ensures it carries all its dependencies, making it environment agnostic. This encapsulation aligns perfectly with the cloud-native tenet of consistent, reproducible deployments across different environments—a developer's local setup, a staging environment, or a production cloud cluster.

Yet, Docker's influence isn't restricted to merely offering a packaging mechanism. Its impact on the operational aspects of cloud-native systems is profound. Orchestration, a fundamental requirement in cloud-native architectures, deals with service deployment, scaling, and management. While Docker introduced Swarm as its native orchestrator, the community largely gravitated towards Kubernetes, a powerful orchestration platform born out of Google's expertise in running containers at scale. Docker integrated Kubernetes' burgeoning dominance, allowing developers to use Kubernetes while staying within the Docker ecosystem. This integration underlines Docker's adaptability and commitment to serving as a foundational pillar in the cloud-native domain.

Beyond the architectural and operational spheres, Docker has also catalyzed a cultural shift, echoing the cloud-native ethos of agility and continuous improvement. Docker has democratized containerization, rendering it accessible to developers, operations teams, and even non-technical stakeholders. This democratization fosters a culture of collaboration, where cross-functional teams can work in unison, sharing Docker images, ensuring consistency, and iterating rapidly. This culture dovetails with the cloud-native emphasis on DevOps practices, where development and operations teams collaborate closely to ensure rapid, consistent, and reliable deployments.

Furthermore, as the cloud-native landscape evolves, there's a growing emphasis on observability and monitoring. Given the distributed nature of cloud-native systems, gaining visibility into operational metrics, logs, and traces is paramount. With its rich ecosystem, Docker integrates seamlessly with tools like Prometheus, Grafana, and ELK Stack, enabling comprehensive monitoring and observability. This integration ensures that Dockerized applications can be monitored, debugged, and optimized in real-time, aligning with the cloud-native principle of proactive system management.

It's also worth noting that the cloud-native terrain, while characterized by its emphasis on the cloud, also acknowledges the importance of edge computing. Here, Docker's lightweight, consistent, and portable nature shines again. Docker containers are ideal for edge deployments, where resources might be constrained, and consistent, reproducible deployments are crucial. By facilitating such deployments, Docker further cements its position in the cloud-native narrative, showcasing its versatility across diverse computing environments.

Additionally, the modern software development landscape is incomplete without touching upon security and compliance aspects. In alignment with cloud-native best practices, Docker promotes immutable infrastructures, where containers are never patched in place but replaced with updated versions. This approach reduces the attack surface, ensures consistency, and facilitates traceability—key tenets in the cloud-native security paradigm.

In conclusion, Docker's position in the cloud-native landscape is multifaceted, profound, and transformative. It's not just a tool that introduced the world to containerization but a catalyst that has reshaped architectural patterns, operational practices, and organizational cultures. Docker's symbiotic relationship with the cloud-native ethos ensures that Docker's relevance and influence will only grow as the latter evolves. Understanding Docker's role, capabilities, and integrations is paramount for organizations and developers treading the cloud-native path. It's a beacon that guides them through the complexities of modern software development, ensuring that they can leverage the full potential of cloud platforms while staying agile, resilient, and scalable. Docker, in essence, is the linchpin that holds the vast, intricate tapestry of cloud-native systems together, steering them toward a future of limitless possibilities.

The road ahead for Docker

In software development, few technologies have had as much impact in such a short span as Docker. From its debut to the present day, Docker has revolutionized how developers think about, package, and deploy applications. The success of Docker can be largely attributed to its user-friendly interface, portability, and promise of "Build Once, Run Anywhere." Yet, as with any technological marvel, the journey never truly ends; it merely transforms. As Docker sits at this transformative juncture, one can't help but ponder its trajectory in the coming years. This section delves into the prospective future of Docker, considering technological advancements, emerging trends, and the evolving needs of the developer community.

To begin, Docker's future seems intertwined with the rise of serverless computing. Serverless, or Function-as-a-Service (FaaS), is a cloud-native development model that allows developers to focus on individual functions without worrying about the underlying infrastructure. With platforms like AWS Lambda and Azure Functions leading the charge, one might wonder where Docker fits in. The answer lies in the concept of containerized serverless environments. Tools such as AWS Fargate offer serverless computing for containers, allowing developers to leverage Docker's portability with serverless scalability. In the coming years, it's plausible that Docker will further integrate with such platforms, providing developers with a seamless experience of containerized serverless computing.

The road ahead for Docker is also paved with the promise of enhanced security. As container adoption grows, so do concerns about security vulnerabilities. Docker continuously evolves its security posture, with features like secure orchestration, image signing, and runtime confinement. Future versions of Docker will likely prioritize zero-trust security models, ensuring robust isolation between containers, enhancing image scanning capabilities, and integrating more closely with enterprise security solutions. Such advancements will address current concerns and bolster Docker's position in mission-critical applications across sectors like finance, healthcare, and defense.

Another exciting dimension in Docker's journey is the potential for greater AI and ML integration. As artificial intelligence and machine learning projects become mainstream, there's an increasing need for reproducible environments that can manage vast datasets, complex dependencies, and heavy computation workloads. Docker's inherent capability to create consistent environments positions it as an ideal tool for AI/ML projects. Future iterations of Docker might offer optimized images for AI frameworks, GPU support enhancements, and integrations with AI platforms like TensorFlow and PyTorch. Such features will democratize AI development, allowing a broader spectrum of developers to dip their toes into the AI/ML realm with the power and simplicity of Docker.

Interoperability is another frontier Docker is set to explore more profoundly. With the proliferation of cloud platforms and the growth of edge computing, there's a tangible need for tools that ensure consistent performance across diverse environments. With its promise of environment-agnostic deployment, Docker is well poised to champion this cause. It's conceivable that Docker will enhance its tooling to offer more granular performance metrics across platforms, facilitate smoother migrations between clouds, and provide optimized support for edge devices, from IoT gadgets to autonomous vehicles.

Furthermore, Docker's future might see a deeper foray into the world of stateful applications. Traditionally, Docker and stateful applications, like databases, had a somewhat complex relationship due to data persistence and performance concerns. However, with advancements in persistent storage solutions and Docker's own features like volumes, this relationship is becoming more harmonious. It's anticipated that Docker will further simplify the deployment and scaling of stateful applications, offering tools and best practices that ensure data integrity, backup, and high availability.

Beyond these technological avenues, Docker's path is also charted by community-driven innovations. The Docker ecosystem thrives on its vibrant community of developers, enthusiasts, and industry experts. As this community grows and diversifies, Docker will likely incorporate user-driven features, from niche use-case optimizations to integrations with emerging tools. These community-centric innovations will ensure Docker remains agile, responsive, and in-tune with the ever-evolving needs of its user base.

Lastly, as with any tech stalwart, Docker's journey will be characterized by continuous education and advocacy. As new developers enter the fold and organizations embark on digital transformation, Docker will amplify its efforts in education, offering comprehensive documentation, interactive tutorials, and community events. This focus on knowledge dissemination will bolster Docker's adoption and ensure its users harness the platform's full potential.

In conclusion, Docker's horizon is vast, dynamic, and brimming with opportunities. Whether serverless computing, enhanced security, AI integrations, or community-driven features, Docker's trajectory promises innovation, adaptability, and relentless growth. As developers and organizations anticipate the future, they can rest assured that Docker, with its legacy of revolutionizing software deployment, will continue to pioneer, adapt, and elevate, guiding the world of software development into new realms of excellence.

CONCLUSION

Recap of the primary points covered in the e-book

As this e-book explains, learning Docker has been an extensive investigation of one of the most revolutionary technologies of the last few years. From its beginnings to its potential future, the e-book covered Docker's nuances, benefits, uses, and best practices to give readers a comprehensive grasp of the technology. As we get closer to the end, it makes sense to go over some of the most important topics that were covered in detail, giving the reader a summary that helps them understand everything.

Fundamentally, Docker introduced the idea of containerization, which changed the software industry. Containerization isolates an application and its dependencies within a 'container,' as opposed to traditional virtualization, which necessitates simulating whole operating systems. As we have discussed, there are many advantages to this technology. Because it guarantees consistency in many contexts, the traditional developer grievance—"It worked on my machine!"—becomes almost nonexistent. Additionally, it promotes speed and efficiency by streamlining the development, testing, and manufacturing cycles.

Now that you know what Docker is, the e-book went into detail about its origins and development, showing how it went from being a simple concept to becoming a standard in the industry. Another important topic was the architecture of Docker, which gave readers information on the client, daemon, and crucial function of Docker registries. The focus was on Docker objects, which are the building blocks of the Docker ecosystem and include images, containers, networks, and volumes.

The technical deep dive proceeded with a detailed examination of the installation procedure. The section emphasized the requirements for setting up Docker and then explained the specific installation procedures for Windows, Mac OS, and Linux. To ensure that the installation went well, there was a section devoted to verifying the setup, which is an important step for both novice and experienced coders.

In later chapters, Docker images—one of its most potent features—took the stage. Through an e-book, the intricacies of Docker Hub—the open registry for Docker images—and its potential applications for developers were examined. Advanced subjects include using Dockerfile to generate custom images and image production best practices made sure readers have all they needed to produce secure and effective Docker images for their applications.

After guiding us through Docker, the e-book moved on to operational topics like starting and stopping containers, gaining access to logs, and the ever-important subject of troubleshooting. A thorough examination of persistent storage and volumes became essential to ensuring that applications preserved data as needed. Alongside, networking and container linking supported the more advanced applications' architectures.

But Docker's real strength is in its orchestration and scalability, areas that Docker Compose and Docker Swarm discussed in great detail. The readers were exposed to the world of multi-container applications, from creating a docker-compose.yml file to scaling with Docker Compose. The experimentation with Docker Swarm also revealed opportunities for considerably larger application scaling.

Continuous Integration and Continuous Deployment, often called CI/CD, are fundamental to the modern development ecosystem, and the e-book did a great job of incorporating Docker into the subject matter. We looked at how Docker may support consistent testing and deployment operations and be a key component of CI/CD pipelines. Investigating the hot-reloading functionality, which enables effective local development using Docker, added to the richness of the discussion.

But there are always difficulties with technology. This e-book outlined the best practices for secure containerization and, more crucially, did not hold back when describing the security risks related to Docker. Deeply exploring practical applications, the e-book covered the function of Docker in microservices architecture, optimization techniques utilizing multi-stage builds, and drew on the extensive knowledge of expert users to offer priceless advice.

Ideas come to life through stories and real-world applications. Based on this assumption, the e-book explored and extracted insights from industry-wide Docker implementations that have been successful. These stories offered a foundational viewpoint on Docker's capabilities, covering everything from difficulties encountered to creative solutions developed.

In the last portions of the e-book, we looked ahead and talked about new developments in the container ecosystem, Docker's role in the broader cloud-native space, and its future directions. The primary topics were growth, innovation, and the never-ending pursuit of faster, smoother, and more efficient software development and deployment processes.

In conclusion, this Docker e-book captured the process of learning the fundamentals to becoming an expert. It sought to provide readers with perspectives, abilities, and information in order to set the groundwork for their future explorations of the dynamic world of containerization and Docker. As we wrap up this summary, we hope that readers—beginners or experts—found value, wisdom, and motivation in these pages, enabling them to move forward with their own Docker-driven projects.

Encouragement to experiment and integrate Docker into development workflows

The only thing that is consistent in the field of software development is change. The constant emergence of new tools, techniques, and best practices forces developers to change and adapt. Docker is one of these inventions that jumps out because it changes how applications are developed, tested, and deployed. But adopting new technologies, such as Docker, requires bravery, curiosity, and adventurous spirit. In order to fully realize Docker's immense potential, developers should read about it theoretically and actively experiment with it and incorporate it into their development processes.

The introduction of Docker into the world of technology provided solutions for several issues that system administrators and developers encountered. This discrepancy between the environments used for development, testing, and production frequently gave rise to the notorious saying, "It works on my machine!" When you use Docker, this problem disappears. By enclosing an application and its dependencies, containers guarantee consistent application operation in many settings. A promise like this promotes smoother deployments, lessens "works on my machine" situations, and facilitates team collaboration. But one must get in and begin traversing in order to enjoy these advantages fully.

The adaptability of Docker is one of its main advantages. Docker has benefits for professionals working in DevOps, data science, and web development. Web developers can use this opportunity to quickly spin up necessary services, like databases or caching servers, without installing them locally. No matter where the code is executed, Docker containers can assist data scientists in making sure that intricate data processing activities with several dependencies work consistently. Furthermore, leveraging tools like Docker Swarm or Kubernetes to grow, maintain, and monitor applications is nothing short of revolutionary for DevOps. Processes can be streamlined and consistency guaranteed by specialists from many areas experimenting with and incorporating Docker into their workflows.

At first, integrating Docker into development processes may appear overwhelming. It is, after all, a departure from conventional wisdom. But Docker's architecture and the large community support make this a worthwhile and doable shift. Environments may be defined clearly and scriptable with Dockerfiles, guaranteeing repeatable and transparent setups. This is further extended by Docker Compose, which makes it simple for developers to define multi-container applications and mimic intricate application structures locally with a few commands. The key to learning Docker is to play around with these tools, try out various setups, and iterate depending on feedback.

Experimentation's power extends beyond its technical aspects, too. Working deeply with Docker allows developers to rethink workflows. Containerized applications, for example, greatly benefit pipelines for Continuous Integration and Continuous Deployment (CI/CD). Every build can be tested in a production-like environment thanks to Docker, which guarantees that any problems are found quickly. The development lifecycle can be streamlined and deployment failures can be significantly decreased with such integration. It is recommended that developers experiment with Docker in their CI/CD workflows in order to find bottlenecks and streamline procedures.

Because of the strong acceptance of Docker by the larger tech community, a robust ecosystem of tools, plugins, and integrations has developed. An abundance of third-party integrations, ranging from security scanners to monitoring systems, are available; all of them are intended to improve Docker's functionality. It is recommended that developers investigate these tools, incorporate them into their processes, and take advantage of the benefits they provide. Every tool and plugin offers a chance to improve, optimize, and elevate development.

Docker offers significant technical benefits, but there's also a psychological component to take into account. A growth attitude is demonstrated by embracing Docker and incorporating it into development workflows. It's a tribute to the ideas of never stopping learning, adjusting to change, and constantly looking for new and improved ways to create and implement software. Understanding a tool is only one aspect of experimentation; another is developing an innovative, inquisitive, and resilient mindset.

In conclusion, Docker invites developers to explore its depths due to its many advantages and revolutionary possibilities. The experience with Docker is about more than just learning its fundamentals; it's also about experimenting, tweaking, and incorporating it into regular processes. Developers who take this approach streamline their operations and set themselves up for lifelong learning and development. Like every technological tool, Docker's actual potential is realized when it's used, not when it's studied. Therefore, the clear call to action for any developer who reads this is to embrace Docker, experiment with it, and incorporate it. The era of containerized applications is just around the corner, offering infinite possibilities, consistent deployments, and simpler development.

Thank you for buying and reading/listening to our book.

If you found this book useful/helpful please take a few minutes

and leave a review on the platform where you purchased our book.

Your feedback matters greatly to us.

www.ingramcontent.com/pod-product-compliance
Lightning Source LLC
Chambersburg PA
CBHW052032150726

48002CB00002B/566